Bethy and the Mouse:
A Father Remembers His Children with Disabilities

Bethy and the Mouse

A Father Remembers His Children with Disabilities

by
Donald C. Bakely

Brookline Books

ISBN 1-57129-035-4

Library of Congress Cataloging-In-Publication Data
Bakely, Donald C.
    Bethy and the Mouse: God's gifts in special packages / by Donald
C. Bakely.
        p.   cm.
    Previous published: Newton, KS : Faith & Life Press, 1985.
    ISBN 1-57129-035-4 (pbk.)
    1. Mentally handicapped children--United States--Family
relationships--Case studies.   I. Title.
HV894.B35   1997
362.3'088'054--dc21   97-3936
                                                           CIP

Interior design and typography by Erica L. Schultz.

Printed in Canada by Best Book Manufacturing, Louiseville, Quebec.

5 4 3 2 1

Published by
BROOKLINE BOOKS
P.O. Box 1047
Cambridge, Massachusetts 02238
Order toll-free: 1-800-666-BOOK

This book is dedicated to:

- The God who was wise enough to give us Beth at a time in our lives when we really would rather not have had another child;

- Jeanne, my wife,

  whose special love, combined with her fears, agonies, and work, have helped so many of us to find an extra warmth in our lives;

- Our other children, Paul, Steve, Claudia, Pete, and Lois,

  whose immediate delight over Beth's life, whose absolute acceptance, overpowering help, and constant love for Beth so beautifully lifted our spirits and our load;

- The "Mouse" (our son, Matthew),

  who died before Beth was born, but who would have been delighted with her company and her antics;

- The gang at the Infant Development Center in Johnson County, Kansas,

  who not only saw who Beth *was,* but who she could be; who studied, trained, taught, opened doors, pushed, encouraged, and loved Beth, and who lifted, taught, and encouraged us as a family;

- And to the rest of us on God's earth

  who find ourselves retarded in the love we give and the accomplishments we would like to achieve, yet attempt to grow more in what we give to others; who realize that we, too, are special and have special gifts yet to offer to those in need.

Contents

PART II: THE "MOUSE"

Foreword

How brief is the time from diapers to kindergarten! The years have passed so swiftly since we first met Bethany.

How well I remember her dear daddy, Don, sheltering her in his large hands. How tiny she was as she and her parents entered our world at the Infant Development Center in Shawnee Mission, Kansas, five years ago. Four weeks of age and eight pounds of dynamite—none of us knew yet how our lives would intertwine.

Jeanne—a super mom! So sweet, so steady, so helpful to the other moms, yet hurting so inside for her little daughter.

Don—an inspiration to all—so strong—so vivacious—so deep and caring, not only for Bethany but for all the other children, too.

Bethany—a tiny rosebud of a person who gazed intently at us all. She would never know the concern we felt. She was so frail and gained so slowly.

There is no more exciting adventure than to join hands with a family and fight together for the life and the future of their little child. We crawled inside each other, we cried together, and we embraced each other in joy with each step forward.

A label—Down syndrome—can say so much, yet so little. The label says *retarded, slow, floppy, dull, different, special education.* "They" said it couldn't be done. At times *we* said it couldn't be done. But Beth seemed to say, "Look at me. I'm a person. Let me try. I can do it!"

When her medical chart said, "Failure to thrive," we worried.

When she reached out and pulled her daddy's beard, we laughed.

When she walked alone, we cheered.

When she called pancakes, "cake cakes," we laughed.

When she threw a tantrum like any other two-year-old, we quietly cheered.

When she called herself "Beckany Blecklick," so did we.

When she entered the mainstreamed preschool, we prayed.

When she passed the entrance exam for kindergarten, we told everyone we knew about it.

And when she hugged us for the last time on her graduation day, we were devastated, but oh, so proud!

The Infant Development Center and Preschool serves developmentally disabled children between birth and five years of age. We offer therapy and education to children, and support and information to parents. The staff includes a program director, registered physical therapists, speech pathologists, early childhood education teachers, and a pediatric consultant. The pediatrician examines each child, counsels with parents, reports to primary physicians, and serves as advisor to the staff.

Treatment, home programs, and parent groups are an ongoing process as staff and family work together with and for each child. The children are evaluated by the team every six months, and a conference is held with the family so that the Individual Program Plan (I.P.P.) and goals may be formulated. You will see these plans placed chronologically through the book interspersed with Don's poems.

The reports are of two types: the professional evaluation done by the staff (the I.P.P.), and the daily comments, feelings, and personal reflections of the staff concerning Bethy, her family, and other influences on her life. We thought those who work professionally with children would be interested in following her technical progress.

What does the future hold for our Bethany? No one knows for certain. But we believe in her and in other children like her. Bethany will make it. Our hope is that those she meets now will do what her family has always done—and it's so easy—just love her and give her time.

— LEE ANN BRITAIN, *Director*
Infant Development Center
Shawnee Mission Medical Center

Introduction

Our family has had twice as many retarded children as almost any other family around. We had two: "Bethy"—Bethany Flagg Bakely, our seventh child, was born June 14, 1976, and still hangs around the house. The "Mouse"—Matthew David Bakely, our fifth child—was born March 10, 1960, and died September 7, 1965. This book is about them.

It's more about Bethy simply because I started writing about her on the night she was born, and I keep a running commentary on her as I watch her grow. It's less about the "Mouse" because I had only written a few things about him while he lived, and because I no longer have the luxury of watching his growth, pain, moods, and joys each day. In the years since his death, of course, I've lost so much of him from my mind. So, a small bit of him (whatever I could dredge up from my memory and the memories of my wife, Jeanne, our other children, and folks who knew him) is included in this book.

The difference between Matthew and Bethy, in some ways, is astronomical. Matthew was microcephalic (he was born with an abnormally small brain). Jeanne had food poisoning during her second month of pregnancy with him. We had gotten some bad chicken while we were camping and it made us all severely ill. We have never known for sure that the sickness was a major contributor in Matthew's condition, but it surely seemed like a logical culprit. At any rate, Matthew was born with a portion of his brain either missing or at least seriously underdeveloped.

His condition was obvious at birth. He required constant care. He could never sit up by himself, walk, talk, chew, or purposely hold anything in his hand. Yet he wasn't just mush. He was an exciting, wonderful, loving person inside that non-working body. He suffered much pain, and was sick—often to the edge of death. He was great agony to us, but he was greater joy.

In the 1960s, there wasn't much help for him. Professionals knew little about his condition and were cautious about using their time on a person with a condition that they knew so little about. I searched through university and professional libraries in an effort to learn as much as I could about this condition and its potential, but all I could find were a few fairly useless, non-encouraging paragraphs.

As a family, we surrounded him with love. We spent hour after hour searching for those things which would give him the faintest glimmer of progress. We exercised him, played, talked, explained, and worked with him for his whole lifetime. In fact, it took two years of working with him every day to teach him to say the simple sound, "O."

But when he did it—when he finally did it—we knew at that moment that he wanted to get out of that prison of his as badly as we wanted to get him out! We were so thrilled! Two years, every day, and it finally paid off!

The professionals had told us that he could never do this. They said that he couldn't possibly control the effort and the mechanics which would allow him to produce a speaking sound. But he did.

When we took him back to the professionals to show them what he could do, they asked us how long it took us to teach him that little trick—and told us to come back when he had conquered "m" or "p."

We didn't go back to them anymore. It just seemed that it was going to be harder to teach them, than it was to teach him.

We started working with him on the sound "I," but he died before we got him that far.

Paul, our eldest, was fourteen when the "Mouse" died. Lois, the youngest, was two: three years younger than the "Mouse." They were all children then, but they were proud of their brother, and very involved in his progress. Their pride was very contagious, and their feelings about him rubbed off on all who met them.

"Mouse" (we called him that because he was so small) died when he was five, three months after we moved from New Jersey to Kansas. He didn't know what life was like without love. That's a pretty neat deal. Few people get to experience life that way.

Bethy is a totally different case. In fact, she's much more like the other kids in our family than she is like Matthew. If we ranged them on a scale of similarities, with Matthew as a 1 and the other kids as 10s, Bethy would be closer to an 8 or 9.

Jeanne and I were in our late forties when Bethy was born. The first six had come in the space of twelve years. The youngest was thirteen when Bethy was born. As you can imagine, Bethy was known, around our house, as the "shock of our lives."

Bethy's condition was not as obvious as Matthew's at her birth. We knew, of course, that there was a strong chance, because of our ages, that she'd be born with Down syndrome, so it didn't come as a total shock to us. And having had the "Mouse," the possibility of her being retarded wasn't a revolting or terribly fearful thought to us.

Because of some problems, Bethy was born by Caesarean section. They let me in the operating room, next to Jeanne, while it happened. I tried to avoid watching them make the initial cuts because I didn't want to see them cut this special woman and because, as this was a new experience for me, I wasn't sure how I'd react. You see, I'm an ex-paratrooper, did a lot of fighting, was in trouble with the law, and was kicked out of home and school when I was seventeen. I am about six feet tall and weigh 200 pounds. The idea of sliding to the floor in a dead faint while they cut her was totally unappealing to me.

But Linda, a nurse friend of ours, was with us during the operation. As they started to cut, she called me to come watch, and I couldn't very well refuse. So I watched.

It was fantastic! A miracle! They cut through the layers, and when they got to the baby, a nurse pulled out just her legs, spread them like a wishbone, and shouted to me, "It's a girl." (I had hoped for a more delicate first view of my daughter!)

After they cleaned her up, they immediately handed her to me. This squishy little thing was ours! And I loved her—right then.

After a moment of introducing her to the fine art of snuggling and hugging, I held her out to get a good look at her. And there were the signs. Those "Downsy" eyes, the bent pinky fingers, the lifeline all the way across the hand.

I asked the doctor if she had Down's. He wasn't sure, so he and Linda took her away and in twenty minutes came back with the report, "She has Down's."

Dr. Ken and Linda were good friends, so they were feeling dejected for us. But I had already had twenty minutes to think about it, so when they made the announcement, I was already feeling better about it than they were. After all, they had never had the wonderful experience of Matthew.

She was our daughter and I felt that God had ways of turning all this into a blessing. After I was reasonably sure that the information was correct, I decided that it was time to tell the rest of the family. They had gathered at our house and were waiting to hear about the baby. I didn't want to telephone because I felt that if they took it hard, it was important for me to be with them. Anyway, Jeanne was still unconscious, so I decided that I could go home for a little while to be with them.

When I got there, I told them that they had a sister, Bethany Flagg Bakely (her mother's maiden name was Flagg), told them her weight, that Mom was OK, and that Beth had Down syndrome.

There was silence for a minute. Lois, thirteen, was only two when Matthew had died, and hadn't had the chance to experience him very much. She began to cry quietly. Then one of the others spoke, "Hey—we can handle *that!*" And I thought, "Bethany Flagg Bakely, you have come to the right house!" And she had!

The older children had already begun to scatter from our home, so Lois, who was the only one still at home, became a second mother to Beth—a friend, mother, sister, playmate—so loving, so proud of her little sister.

Let me quickly introduce the rest of our children.

Paul was born in 1951. At the moment of this writing, he is working for Cross-Lines (the inner city church agency of which I am executive director). He left college to marry and is now going back to finish his degree.

Steve, born in 1953, was a music major until Bethy was born, then changed to music therapy. He just finished his internship in a state mental hospital in Texas, and is working at a group home for mentally handicapped adults in the Kansas City area.

Claudia, born in 1955, is a graduate nurse, married, and has been working with birth-disabled babies in the infant intensive care unit at the Kansas University Medical Center.

Pete, born in 1958, is an actor with the Missouri Repertory Theater, and is working on his acting degree at the University of Missouri.

Lois, born in 1963, just graduated from high school, made her first parachute jump, and is majoring in art therapy at Emporia State College in Emporia, Kansas.

They all were in the National Honor Society and are all working, or have worked, their own way through college. Each one's adventures would fill a book.

They are all wonderful with Bethy. Naturally, this is all a great source of comfort for Jeanne and myself. We know that we aren't alone in rearing Bethy, and we know that with brothers and sisters like Bethy's, we don't have to fear for her future.

The rest of our relatives and friends have been wonderful. Many of them remembered Matthew, and remembered what he had meant to them, and remembered how much he meant to, and did for, us. They had watched us all through Matthew's life, and they knew, from our history, that Bethy would not be a crushing blow to us. They already knew that remarks such as "Oh, you poor things" and "We're so sorry" were inappropriate. They didn't have to go through that whole awkward thing of "What do we say? How do we handle this?" They were able to read our joy and commitment from the start, and so were at ease with us and with Bethy.

My father, who never got his rough edges sanded down, sent us a note when he heard of Bethy's birth and of her Down syndrome. It said, "Just think, Bud [his name for me], some families never even get to have one retarded child. You and Jeanne were lucky enough to get two."

He was right. And the reason he knew we'd feel that way was that somewhere along the line he and my mother had set the tone that helped us to see Bethy and the "Mouse" as joy, and as special gifts in slightly different packages.

Not only is Bethy much different from Matthew, conditions surrounding the retarded are different today than they were when Matthew was alive. As recently as the '40s, Down's children were hustled off to state institutions, often to vegetate. Their life span was predicted to be about fifteen years. They were thought of and referred to as "Mongolian idiots."

Things are very different now. Early intervention is common. For example, Bethy started school at the Infant Development Center (now connected with the Shawnee Mission Medical Center in Johnson County, Kansas) when she was one month old. For the first five years of her life, she went several half-days per week. At first, they worked on muscle development and physical progress. Instead of having the traditional chubby little mushy-muscled body, she's very sturdy, strong, healthy (but short. They didn't seem to be able to do anything about "tall"). She still has some problems with balance and coordination. She seems to conquer each problem just a little later than other children, but eventually, she does conquer them. She's normal in most things. Where her condition does hold her back, she catches up. Her speech, comprehension, and social skills are fairly close to normal.

Starting public school this fall, in regular classes, with no special education, will be an experiment for the school system as well as for her and us. But things have changed. As a society we have learned much about kids like her. We must get ready for them. There are lots of Bethys coming along, and with our help, they can be useful, producing citizens, We need to make up our minds that there will be no more scrap heaps made up of people like her.

Of course, we, as a family, are nervous about her going to "regular" school. The schools are, too. Bethy will be a first for them. How will the teachers handle her? Will she be looked at as another problem? How will the other kids treat her? Wrong attitudes can hurt her a lot, can cause a very important experiment to fail, and can hurt thousands who follow her.

We and the school are both open to change. If we find that we are pushing her too far and too fast, we will adapt. If we find that she needs special education classes, of course we will shift that way.

Our hopes for her are that she will acquire and develop the kinds of skills and attitudes that she will need to live life at its fullest. We also hope that she will be able to live independently, that she will find some special skill or gift which will be unique to her, and that she will see herself as a giver—a contributor—not just a receiver. We hope to help her find the faith, personality, and strength to be able to deal with the confusions of life, and to be as victorious as possible over the temptation to feel badly about herself. Of course, these are the things we want for our other kids as well. We even harbor hopes that Bethy will eventually graduate from high school. We realize that this is more and more a possibility.

The chances of our living to see her get through her twenties are getting slimmer and slimmer. After all, we are both in our fifties now. For kids like her, the twenties are usually pretty formative years. Job skills, independent living training, etc., are usually still a large part of their lives during those years. So, seeing her "settled" is probably a luxury that we won't have. As I said before, we're not too worried about that. Her brothers and sisters will be around when we're not. And so will lots of others who care.

Many agencies, institutions, and individuals are studying and learning about mentally handicapped persons. Doors are being opened on their behalf. Another encouraging note is that so many of the people who are working with handicapped persons today are doing it out of a sense of commitment. They seem excited about what these persons are learning and accomplishing. Very few of the people who are looking to specialize in working with the retarded seem to be just "looking for a job." We have been impressed with the faculty, students, and staffs of many of the schools which prepare students to work with retarded persons.

The church, too, is seeing this work as a part of its ministry. I speak several hundred times a year around the country. It always thrills me when I go to churches like the First United Methodist in Lawrence, Kansas, or the First Christian Church in Beloit, Kansas, where I see many retarded persons taking an active and natural part in the worship and programs of the church. Valley View and Bristol Hill United Methodist churches in the Kansas City area have special programs and services for the retarded persons and families in their areas, as lots of other churches do.

Businesses are adapting to the handicapped in various ways. Job training, independent and semi-independent living situations, research facilities, and a myriad of services for the retarded and their families have made this a much better world for the retarded and for all of us. And, of course, so have places like the Infant Development Center, where speech, music, art, occupational, physical, and many other kinds of therapies are mixed with love and skills in such a way as to help handicapped persons become joyful and useful persons.

Many people are breaking the molds and changing many minds about the handicapped persons. Look, if you are going to have a retarded child, this is as good a time as any. So, go right ahead. Two hundred years ago was a rotten time. Fifty years ago, folks were stashing retarded people away in institutions. Twenty-five years ago many were being hidden away in their homes, and families were ashamed to admit that their child was retarded.

But today it's changing. We are learning how to turn agonies into triumphs, and we are all better for it. Today I see parents, families, communities, and helpers with intense pride in the achievements of their retarded friends. If you want to see this attitude at work, go to the next Special Olympics competition that you hear about. It may just be the most fun-filled, exciting, encouraging day of your life.

Finally, a word to—and about—other parents of retarded children. I must confess that when I am with other parents of retarded children—and especially when I am asked to speak to groups of parents—I get nervous. There are so many different feelings and approaches to deal with. Some feel cursed. Some are overwhelmed with the changes that these children make in their lives. Some are touchy about feelings which disagree with theirs.

I listen to some and I wonder if that's the way I'm really supposed to feel. I ask myself if other parents see me as slightly out of touch with reality and with present-day knowledge. I also wonder if my expressed feelings cause them pain.

Sometimes when I listen to other parents, I try to reevaluate some of the things I think about Bethy and the "Mouse," and I wonder if I am just psyching myself into all these positive thoughts. Maybe I am. I guess we all have our ways of coping. We parents seem to need some kind of response that works for us.

As for me, I've often said that when God invented Down syndrome, it was one of God's best days. What God wanted for us was the closest expression of pure, unadulterated love since Jesus. I think that if I had to choose a child to raise, at my age, I'd choose a child with Down syndrome. The kid brings me more happiness and joy than a roomful of somebody else's puppies.

Now and then people say, "Of course you feel that way about Bethy. She's healthy, bright, in regular classes in regular school. You've hardly got a retarded kid at all."

I hear that and agree. Bethy is easy to take. But do remember that the "Mouse" was also our child and that we were thankful to have him, too. We felt enriched and blessed by his life.

There are lots of Bethanys and Matthews in this world. We need them. They seem to bring out such good things in us, once we get to know them. They give us a special quality in our lives. They draw us out of our selfishness. They inspire us. They give us much more than they take. This world would lose so much without them.

To the many like Bethy and the "Mouse," and to those who care for them, I'm glad you happened to us. I thank God for his wisdom in sending you our way.

The word "retarded"

I am not unaware of the problems surrounding the use of the word "retarded." Having spoken to many folks about it, I find no clear consensus on the proper word to use. I do, however, find clear opinions. Some folks are absolutely insistent that the proper term is "developmentally disabled." Others insist that the only term is "mentally handicapped."

Frankly, I just don't know which term is correct—or least offensive. I find great disagreement and often intense feelings surrounding the many different terms, and those feelings are spread out among parents, clients, professionals, and other interested persons.

I recognize that we are, at this point, in a transitional stage regarding our terms. Not being much of a prophet, I don't know which word or phrase is eventually going to win. Frankly, when Bethy is old enough to think about the terms and to deal with them, I think she is going to be equally offended by being labeled "mentally handicapped" or "developmentally disabled" as by being labeled "retarded."

All I can say is that I'm in a quandary about the proper term. I use several in this book—whichever felt right at the time.

I'm not writing the book as a professional in the field. I'm writing it as a father—a father who desperately loves his little girl and who still loves his son, even though the "Mouse" has been dead for almost twenty years.

— DONALD C. BAKELY

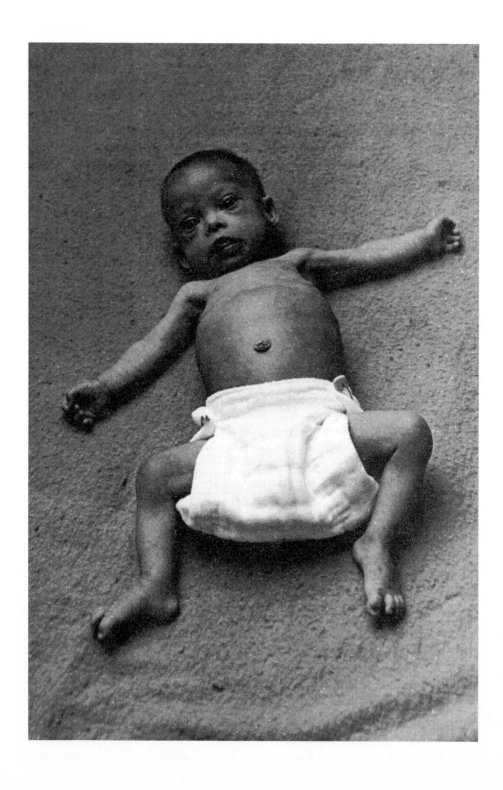

PART I

Bethy

Bethany Flagg Bakely

Special gifts

We keep looking for gifts in regular packages.
If I wrapped one in newspaper
    or in a brown paper bag,
or if it was something I found in a field
    instead of the shelf of a store,
it wouldn't seem as *legitimate* a gift.

If it cost me feeling instead of money,
it would seem somehow not as worthy.
Maybe that's because
    we can't transfer
    our feelings
    to others
    as easily
    as money.

Well—
Beth is one of those special gifts of God
in different wrapping.
She's a gift
    from God's feelings.

Maybe the hardest thing about receiving a gift in special packaging
    isn't understanding the gift
    or understanding that it *is* a gift—
Maybe the problem is
    that we don't know how
    to explain the feelings behind it
to those who only look for regular packages.

You're WHAT?

(November, 1975)

You say
funny things have been happening
to your period lately?

Well, we *are* getting the right age
for menopause—*a little* young,
but sometimes it happens at our age.
And menopause
is at least better than that *other* possibility—.

Still—have it checked out.

We wouldn't want it to be a problem
that was dangerous to you.

(December, 1975)

I

Pregnant!!!
Pregnant!!!
You think you are pregnant???

Not *now!*
Not at *our* age!!
Our kids are almost grown—.
We were just talking about your finally being able
        to travel with me,
        sharing the things
        I only get to see by myself.

Pregnant??
It *couldn't* be.

I don't even remember being
    careless in our love
    —do you?

II

Lord,
Let me explain something to you.
Are you listening?
Are you paying any attention?
I'd like this to be clear to you!
Hear this—
If you'd really like to know,
we'd rather not!!!
If there's a chance,
any chance,
that she's not pregnant,
I'd appreciate it
if
you'd tip the scales that way!

Not now. Not again.

Who needs to have raised one large family
and then one only child?
Who needs 45 years of P.T.A.?
Who needs to look forward
to another kid
becoming a teenager?
(When this one's 13, I'll be 61!)

You are known for your kindness.
How about spilling a little on us now—
in our hour of need?
Look,
if you can't arrange kindness,
I'll take some simple *justice*.

III

Yet, Lord,
    whatever—
of course we yield to your wisdom.

You've been in business a long time
and have always impressed me
with your wisdom—
even when you have interfered with my life.
And when we have disagreed in the past
    you always seem to outsmart me
and your way turned out right and best.
So whatever happens, we accept.
And we will accept with joy
—and trust.

Even though we'd rather not go through this,
we will—if it happens—
and we'll pull out all the stops,
    and do our best,
    and love it well,
    and make it warm,
    and things will be OK.

You know that we'll be ready, Lord.
It's just that it's kind of a shock.
But we'll get over the shock
—if it's true—.

I just wanted you to know
that
we'd rather
not!

The Night of Her Birth

I

My baby?
    My brand new Beth?
Down's syndrome???

Why, God?
What in the world is the matter with you?
What is there that gives you jollies
    in creating partial people?
Why?
Did you think things were getting too easy for us?

Damn!!!
    Why??
Anyway,
    why *us?*
Haven't you noticed,
we've *paid* our dues!

Matthew—
    microcephalic
    never able to sit up,
    hold up his head,
    walk, talk, chew, hold anything in his hand
every sickness slamming him to the edge of dying.

Mom-Mom—
    arteriosclerosis, colitis;
    argumentative, confused, pesty, dependent.

Why Beth too?
Why do you want us to spend
the rest of our years
    explaining

training
sheltering
carrying
our last child?

I'm tired tonight,
    and too damned old for this.
We wanted to be free
    to travel, to be without kids,
    to enjoy some years by ourselves.

But you did it to us again,
    didn't you?
Why?
Why *us??*
We don't deserve this!

II

Hey—
I've been thinking, Lord.
Let me rephrase that.

Why *not* us?
We've certainly had
plenty of practice.

And, Lord,
when we get over these first few moments,
    you know we've got the feeling for it.
And come to think of it,
we've got a family that will love her.
We can certainly
surround her with joy.
And that's what you need for her,
isn't it?

Hey—
Matthew did us good,
not evil.
He and Mom-Mom made us grow,
  be patient,
  stretch our love,
  learn about caring,
  and teach others.
And that's the good stuff of life.
They helped us touch other lives
  in a caring kind of way.

Lord,
thanks for reminding me.
We *are* right for this child.
And we are your children,
  committed to your will.

And,
if this is your will,
  it must be good
  —for all of us.

We *will* do what you ask.
And if you think our shared lives can do good for each other,
  that's OK with us.

III

Yeah—why not?
  Why *not* us?
I saw her birth—
  saw them cut my wife
  and wrench this child
  into life.
They let me hold her right away
  and feel her cheeks on mine.
I watched her tiny hands and feet quiver.

Saw her as she struggled to squeeze open her eyes.

I love her already.
I don't care if she's got webbed feet.
She's mine.
And we need
    each other.

I'm still asking,
        why, Lord?
But the question is changed for me.
Why, Lord?
    Why did you choose to bless us again?
Why, of all the possible families,
        did you choose us
        for this armful of love?
I was right before.
We don't deserve this.
        But you have a way of blessing us
        beyond our deserving.

If you had given us the choice,
we would have said no.
and we would have missed
        these moments
        of giving and receiving
        and growing in love.

Thank you, Lord,
for being smarter
        than we are.

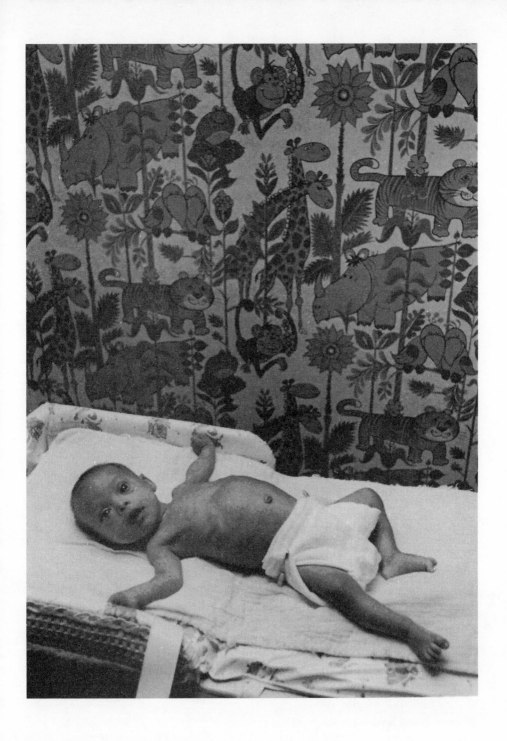

Don't worry about tomorrow

"Don't worry about tomorrow.
      It'll have enough worries of its own."
Jesus
      keeps making sense to me.
It's Beth's tomorrows
that cause us pain.
Who will she be?
What care will she need?
How much pain will others give her?
Will life be embarrassing for her
      —or us?
What will happen to her—tomorrow?
What will happen when *we* die—
Who will love her—tomorrow?

A lot of todays,
coming clumped up,
still in the dark
are called *tomorrows*—
and they have worries
tacked on.

Her tomorrows are frightening.

But if we do
what Jesus advises,
(take no thought of tomorrow)
and just take her each day,
      it's different.

Because *today* she's warm and soft to my touch.
She excites and delights us.
We watch her hands move gently.

Her eyes
    squinch
    in response to love.
She snuggles in the morning
and gently stretches her arms
to feel us beside her.

Her cries are for this moment's pains,
    not for tomorrow's fears.
We watch her try out a new face or sound,
    response, or move;
and today is a day
    full of the joy of our baby.

It's only her tomorrows
    that frighten me.
The todays bring us joy,
    make us anxious to touch her face.

Isn't it a special wisdom
that God
gently slips the tomorrows to us
    one day at a time
and turns them from a clump of fears
into joys and pains
    that we can handle?

INFANT DEVELOPMENT CENTER

Bethany Bakely

1. INDIVIDUAL PROGRAM PLAN—STAFF EVALUATION
4 Weeks—(Excerpt from Physical Therapist's report)

Assessment—A 1-month-old Down's child functioning at approximately the 1 month level in motor skills. She is an alert baby who interacts well with her environment through both her vision and hearing, although she prefers her hearing. She keeps herself content with hand-to-mouth activities and sucking on her fingers. If this does not work she enjoys being hugged and cuddled and snuggles nicely into the arms.

Therapy Plan—Mother and child will meet with Mothers of the Down's syndrome group, and their children, for 1/2 hour and then both Mother and child will be involved in a 1-1/2 hour stimulation session.

Mother was instructed today to:

1. Place the child on her stomach.

2. Use hearing and visual stimulation together and then decrease hearing stimulation to increase visual focusing and tracking,

3. Place the child over a small roll to encourage head lifting via both visual and hearing stimulation and support on forearms.

2. STAFF COMMENTS 1 thru 7 months
Beth—Progress Notes

7-16-76   Beth worked hard at bringing her head up when over the roll. The vibrator seemed to facilitate this. In visual focusing and tracking she did best when the colored balls were paired with the bell. "It's hard, but we're doing better."

9-14-76   Parents indicated no true progress had been made.

10-26-76   Concern re: size and failure to grow.

11-16-76   Mom reports Beth has gained two ounces.

1-3-77   Feeding in supported sitting in high chair. Beth alert and happy today.

2-1-77   Reaching and grasping in supine. Vocalizing more. Bearing more weight on lower extremities. Sitting more erect.

The Down syndrome face

You didn't get much of a nose, Kid.

It looks like somebody
    dropped
the end of a red jelly bean
on your face.

But you *did* get big eyes, Kid.
Big, talkative, commandeering, intense blue (like your Dad!)
eyes.

And that mouth—
that strong, sweet, sloppy, drippy,
turn-me-inside-out-with-a-smile mouth.

And a face just jam-packed with *you*.
You've got Down's, all right.
No question about it.
But right now,
    I couldn't care less
    if you had three legs.
'Cause you're just right for
    huggin', kissin', lovin', watchin',
    and thankin' God for.

It's a *great* face.
And it does so many neat things.

Why did this happen to you/to us?

I think I understand
　　why you happened to us,
But I'm not sure I understand
　　why this happened to you!
Why some tiny chromosome decided to go astray
and why it decided to do it
　　in your body.

If I have trouble understanding it,
so, of course, will you.
Yet the time will come
when you will understand *this—*
that something serious, lasting, and uncorrectable
has completely affected your life.

What if,
　　when those moments come to you,
you aren't as able to accept *that*
as we are able, happy, honored,
to accept *you?*

Is there a way, Child?
Is there a way, Jeanne?
Is there a way, Experts?
Is there a way, Lord,
　　that we can keep her pleased
　　with who she is
rather than depressed
　　about who she is not?

We have the feeling
that it was a special wisdom,
　　and not a special curse,
that made her for this world
　　and put her in our hands.

And we suspect
that there is also
    a grace given to us
    in the whole package
—a grace that corresponds
    to her needs.
The time is coming
when we may need
    to cash some of that in.

Give us that measure
    of wisdom and love
that can surround her
with the kind of acceptance
that can't easily be cracked
when she begins to ask
why this all happened to
                    her.

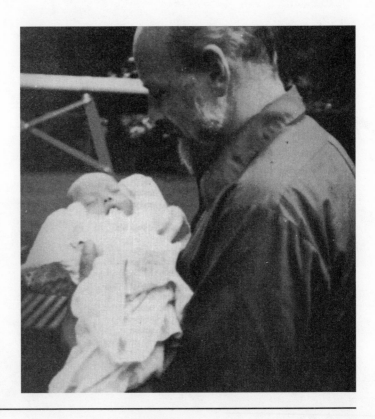

An obstinate baby

"Don't let the world squeeze you into its mold."
I didn't think you knew Scripture, Kid.
But you surely do practice
    that verse.

You are the loviest–most hardheaded,
    sweetest–most obstinate
      bundle of baby
I ever met.

They say it comes with your condition,
and I guess we are going to have to learn
    to live with it,
and even learn
    to like it.

How can somebody your size
insist
    so hard?

You can't talk,
but you surely can communicate
and let your "no's" be known.

Your cantankerousness
is sometimes hard for us to live with,
but somehow I know
it's going to serve you well
as you learn to live in,
    with, and sometimes against your world,
as that world tries to squeeze you
    into its mold,
and as you, in turn, tell that world
    what you'll accept,
    what you are comfortable with,

and how much you are willing to stand.
I'm torn between teaching you to adapt to your world's ways
and not wanting to stifle that special personality
that is uniquely you.

The world has much to learn
from the "don't-push-me" person that you are.

Your insistent ways
may be your best defense in life,
and I'm glad
(I think)
that you have them.

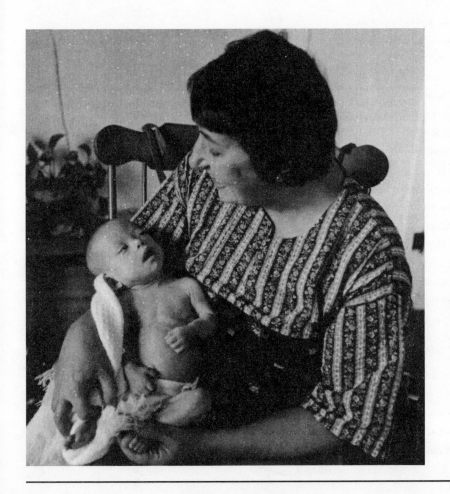

Training your daddy

(Five Months)

You're so new—
yet you've already learned so much.
You know how to use your body,
    eyes,
    mouth,
to give me messages.
You seem to feel some satisfaction
in the way you've trained me.
(I thought I was supposed to be training *you!*)

You lie in the playpen,
    growing weary of the same
    sights and sounds.
I keep making the same two mistakes—
    I seem to always pass by at the wrong moment
    and I let our eyes meet.
Immediately
your eyes flash
that Hi-I'm-adorable-and-cuddly,
    wouldn't-you-like-to-hold-me look.
You have a split second to tell
    if that did the job.
You compute its effectiveness,
sense me passing by,
and the bottom lip (fastest bottom lip in the west),
jumps right out.

It suckers me into watching
    for that fatal one more second
while the body stiffens,
the belly arches up
and the face insists, begs, charms, woos, loves,
    shouts *pick me up!*
And I'm hooked again,

trapped by a seven-pound brute of insistence.

Yeah.
Your infancy training process
is going well, Kid.

And I know who's getting trained!

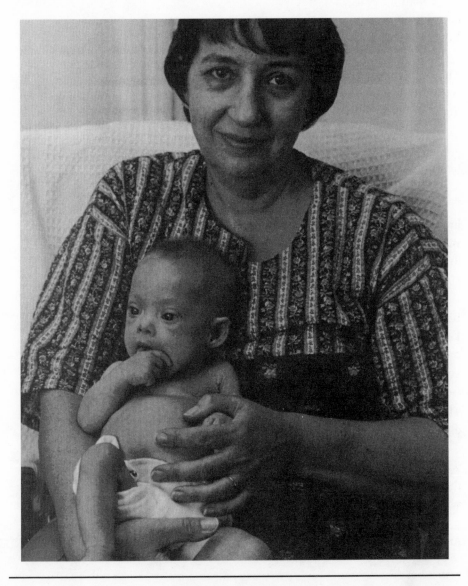

Bonding

(Six Months)

When I hold you,
    tiny woman,
When I hold you,
    the world becomes
    a warmer place.
How did you learn such love
in six short months?

The special moments
when I sit back in my chair
and you lie on my chest
first looking in my eyes, then
    making long senseless noises
        and sentences
    that somehow say
    a lot of special things to me,
are moments
that bind.

(I think I'm glad
    that you can't talk yet,
because—for a while—
I can put loving feelings
behind what I can assume to be
your loving sounds.)

Then,
after we've said
    enough good things
    to each other,
the moment comes
when you tell me the best of all
    without words.
One long,

loving look,
    straight at me,
eye to eye—
lasting 'til you are sure it's said
    and received.
Then the head
lies on my chest
and we belong,
    really belong!
And I know the love is there.

The trust, the comfort,
the way you melt into my body
says we are *friends* and we both know it.
It seals us.
And I *need* that.

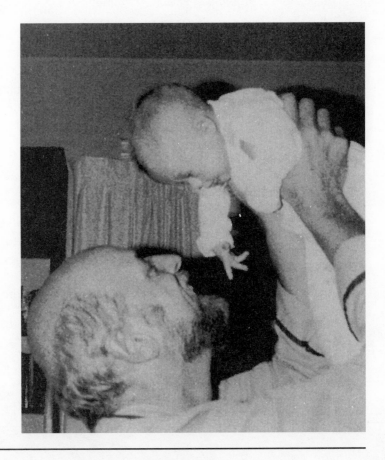

INFANT DEVELOPMENT CENTER

1. INDIVIDUAL PROGRAM PLAN - STAFF EVALUATION

7 Months—Physical Therapist describes Beth as alert and sociable. At this time she:

1. Lifts her head when placed on her stomach.
2. Reaches for toys and faces.
3. Quiets to sounds.
4. Laughs and vocalizes.
5. Shows decreased muscle tone and muscle strength.

Assessment—Beth is a 7-month-old Down's, functioning as follows:

Language .... 5 Months

Cognition (Education/Thinking/Reasoning) ....5–6 Months

Fine motor and perceptual motor (use of hands) ....4 Months

Gross Motor (Large motor skills) . 4-1/2 Months

Self Help, feeding .... 6 Months

Social .... 5 Months

In the past 6 months, Beth has made 4-6 months progress.

Long Term Goal: Placement in preschool when age appropriate.

Short Term Goals:

1. Improve head control and sitting balance.

2. Improve muscle tone and strength.

3. Facilitate reach and grasp.

4. Facilitate better rolling.

2. STAFF COMMENTS 7 to 14 months

2-1-77 Reaching and grasping in supine, Vocalizing more. Bearing more weight on lower extremities. Sitting more erect.

3-1-77 Tolerated supporting on hands in prone over roll.

3-15-77 Marked improvement in past week.

3-22-77 Fussy today—not too cooperative.

3-29-77 Sat alone for 40 seconds!

4-5-77   Using right more than left with reaching. Work on two-handed activities.

5-17-77   Remains in 4-point position if placed for short period of time if lower extremities are stabilized. Standing with hyperextension of knees. Physical assist needed to support self in sitting with hands out to either side. Tilting reactions in prone and supine improved. Protective extension in sitting with some assist.

5-24-77   Beth anticipates object around head in both directions. Protective reactions elicited with assist. Pivots 45 degrees in both directions. Moves a few inches forward to obtain object with some assist. Tilting reactions elicited to right and left in sitting. Send home therapy program for summer.

7 months—Evaluation Day

Big day, Kid!
Big,
    good
        day.
Evaluation day for you
by the people
who have been teaching you
    so much.
Carolyn checks you out,
    questions us,
    tests you.

Social skills—near seven months,
Motor skills—around five months.
    Much progress, thanks to them!

You seem to try so hard;
you make us *so* proud.
Think of it—a baby who *tries!*
Most babies just get to grow.
You have to *strain!*
And you do it.

Next, to the doctor.
Today, finally, you are past ten pounds!
You, the skinny baby
who hardly gained
for months,
    who looked like an ad
    for world hunger.
You—finally—
sturdy, strong,
and out of the woods!

We *are* going to make it.
And you *are* going to stay
     to grow
     and learn
     and teach
     and love
     and share your life
        with us.
It's been a good day, Kid,
and we jumped a lot of hurdles
together.

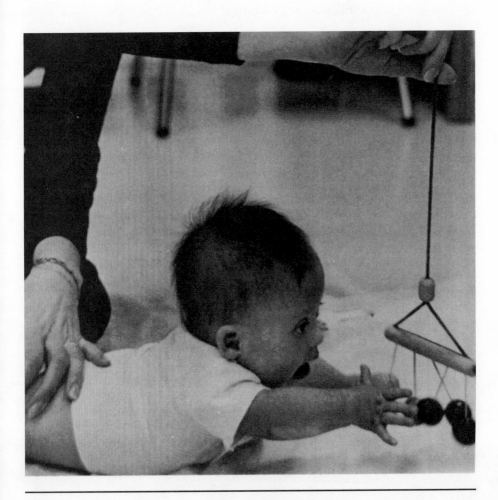

Small pains, large loves

(One Year)

They fit,
so I guess you think
babies' thumbs
and thumbnails
are *supposed* to go up daddies' noses
while daddies are asleep.

I must admit
if I were your size
    and there was a still, sleeping face
    near my lap
I'd think it was a lovely place
to test two jaggedy,
razor-edged, brand new teeth.

After all,
how are you to know
that a single shove
    of one sharp finger
or the clawing act
    of a tiny hand
isn't the way to move the eyelid
so you can see that shiny marble
    that you know
    is behind that little flap of skin?
And yes,
the beard is not supposed
    to rip off.
No—not in large clumps
or in strands of two or three
still attached to my mustache.

A double-handed whack
on my bald head

followed by
     a pint of slobber
     intended as a kiss
and offset by looks of sheer passion
and absolute innocence
tells me that all this
     is love and trust.

Pain for pain's sake hurts.
But the pain that I can stand
     is the pain that comes
     from a pair of your lovin' hands.

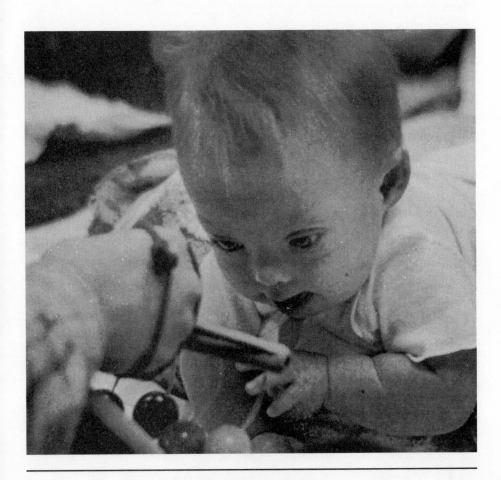

Real beauty

As I drive across Kansas
in the different moments of the year
I'm thankful for the many ways
beauty makes itself known,
and even more thankful that
    somewhere, somehow I was taught
that beauty can be found
in unlikely places.

I love the sharp silhouette
of a once-live tree
when the morning pushes its light through
    to prepare the way for the day.
I find the desolation of eastern Utah
    moving, inspiring, breathtaking.
The beige, cattle-specked hills of Kansas
always touch me with the warmth of their beauty.
And yet,
others have spoken to me in despair
of the emptiness, the boring-ness
of these same things.

I think this happens also with Down's people.

I remember seeing Down's kids before,
and thinking the word "homely."
But that was before you, Beth
    and you, Stacey,
    and you, Jennifer,
    and the rest of Beth's schoolmates
who, since Beth,
have burst into my life.
When I see those sweet gushing mouths,
    those almost left-out noses,

those eyes that are always getting ready
    to do something,
and the rest
of what you come with,
then I am reminded that God, the ultimate artist,
    has a better sense of beauty than we have.
And in you,
God gave us a beauty
that runs amok
    and that moves all up and down
    and in and around our senses.
The special thing
for those of us who have Down's kids
is that God gave us a beauty
    that can be hugged.
And when it's hugged,
it somehow becomes enlarged
    and unique in its power to move.

Beauty was meant to be sensed
and yours is a beauty
that touches me.

Feeding the dog

(One Year)

You're a sneaky little kid, aren't you?
With all our efforts
    to teach you differently,
the dog knows she can count on you
to get the food to her
that you don't like
    (or do like, for that matter).
So at mealtimes,
she sits patiently at the foot of your high chair
    waiting—
and as surely as night follows day,
that little hand
whips the food to the floor.

Even if you like it all,
she knows that her soft whine
will be a signal for you to share.

Sometimes you check our eyes for a "no,"
and while watching us
    and seeing the "no,"
that hand still sneaks food under the tray
    to feed and get cleaned off
    by an anxious tongue.

Your loyalty is commendable
    and clearly established.

And the dog,
    like us,
is glad you came.

INFANT DEVELOPMENT CENTER

1. INDIVIDUAL PROGRAM PLAN—STAFF EVALUATION
14 Months—The early childhood special education teacher describes Beth as alert and happy.

Beth's development scores are:

Assessment—		Gain in 7 mo.
Language	11 Mo.	5 mo.
Social	16 mo.	5 mo.
Feeding	11 Mo.	6 mo.
Cognition	10 Mo.	5–6 mo.
Fine Motor	10-10-1/2 mo.	6–6-1/2 mo.
Gross Motor	9 mo.	4-1/2–5 mo.

Parent Comments—Realistic, pleased with progress. Agree with test results.

2. STAFF COMMENTS—14 to 21 months.

9-12-77   Beth attending to toys and activities today. Observed a word approximation during session. Using spoon with assistance to feed self. Need to work on taking bites of cookie held.

10-3-77   Attended to toys and activities for short span of time. Easily distracted by noise and other children. Removed own socks with verbal and gestural encouragement. Moves forward to obtain object by scooting on hands and right lower extremity with left lower extremity tucked under her in a sitting position. Became cranky when attempts were made to change her to a hands and knees position for creeping.

10-17-77   Beth was easily distracted by other children and checked to see where her mother was. She discriminated ball twice and car once today. She loved looking at the book. We began activities standing but she lasted only a short time—preferred to finish the activities sitting down.

10-31-77   Beth showed spontaneous vocalizations throughout session. She repeated "Hi" throughout. Seemed to enjoy the socialization with Jennifer and Amy.

11-7-77   Beth continues to scoot in sitting. Maintenance of all-4's improved. Comes to stand with assist.

11-28-77 Beth had infected left eye and did not feel well today. Refused most activities or watched others.

12-12-77 Beth appears to be going thru astasia—no weight bearing on lower extremities. Beth was observed to creep reciprocally approximately 3 ft. without putting foot up to scoot. Difficult to interest in tilting activities.

12-19-77 Finger painted Christmas present—Beth did not like activity. Family left early for appointment.

1-9-78 Beth prefers right hand. Dislikes any physical prompts with activities. Imitating dog sound, cow and horse. Stacked 2 blocks one time.

1-9-78 Is creeping with correct reciprocal pattern, with less reversion to scooting in sitting. Still no interest in standing. Did stand briefly at table with therapist's support.

1-26-78 Seen individually for education. Throwing some objects in refusal to "give to worker." Some spontaneous babbling during session—no verbal imitation immediately after stimulus. Imitation of pat-a-cake one time, Responded to "no"—inhibited inappropriate behavior.

2-2-78 Observed more standing—two times independent standing for a few seconds. When presented initially with toy to left she would reach with the right, but when right is restrained for several trials she uses the left more frequently with and without restraint of right.

2-9-78 Independent attempts to get into vertical position with pulling to stand. Reaching with left is increased. More accuracy is observed in releasing with the left also.

2-23-78 Educational one-on-one session. Initial difficulty with sitting at floor table—needing physical assistance to attend and stay seated. Many distractions in the large room. Beth cried and screamed, refusing to cooperate with obstacle course, or any tilting on board, ball, or barrel.

Ego shadows

(Fourteen Months)

I hear myself saying
lots of joy
about you.
And I mean it all.

But there are some shadows, too—
personal shadows for me—
ego shadows, for instance.

Through all my intense pride over being your father,
I have my other moments.
Like
when I talk about you and the "Mouse"
both in one family,
both flowing from me.

I wonder what thoughts
     what conclusions
run through my listener's mind
about *my* defects.

One retarded child in a family draws some sympathy
and support. But two!
Is that excusable?
Does that change sympathy to suspicion?

Two!
     Yes, two—in one family.
What does that say to *them* about me?
     about my sperm?
     about my manhood?

I know it's silly
and unworthy of me
and all that stuff,
but being a person,
I've still got my ego
to keep intact.

Sometimes I feel the need to quickly explain
that my five "normal" children
are "normal."
all in the tops of their classes—
    strong
    healthy
    college-bound
    concerned
    beneficial to humankind
    loving
    children-to-be-proud-of-types.

Sometimes I wish I could bring along
one of my over-six-feet sons
or one of my bright, attractive daughters
just to show
that my sperm worked well
most of the time.

Sometimes I find myself wanting to explain
    that my wife had severe food poisoning during the second month
    of her pregnancy with the "Mouse,"
to explain that it was no weakness in us
but just one of those strange, once-in-a-million happenings
that happened to us
    —twice.
Sometimes I catch myself wanting to mention
    my paratrooper days, degrees, honors,
just to remind others
that the retardation was a fluke—
    and doesn't run in the family.

Sometimes I want to mention
    my brighter-than-me
    kinder-than-me
    more sensitive-than-me
    wife,
so that when these things are added up
you will know
that two retarded children
throw no reflection on us.

That's my ego at work.
And while I want to share the joy of my two "special" children,
I'm not always sure that I want to do it
    at the expense of my ego.

Damn.
    That's foolish!
But it's there—
in the shadows.

You brighten up the place

We sure do love you, Pumpkin Face.
You have a way of throwing joy
into
    any kind of a day.

That face of yours
    brightens up all the darknesses.
Your smile
can happy up
a whole crowd.

And who you are
    each today
knocks the fears out of who you will be
    in the distant tomorrows.

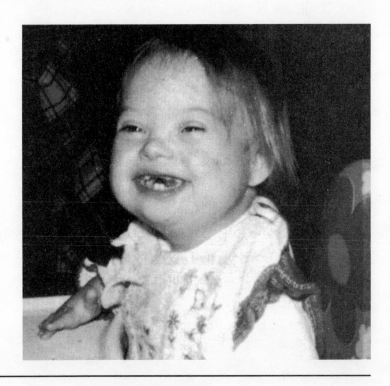

Moving to music

(Sixteen Months)

I think we've got
the Mahalia Jackson
of the Down's set.

Beth was itchy after supper.
I got out the guitar
to play some folk and country music.
She smiled.
Then a gentle tapping of her hand
began on her high chair.

The little body started to move
in a soft, quiet rhythm,
    close and intentionally to the beat.
She danced while sitting,
gently lifting one bottom cheek
then the other.

Singing sounds came next—
    more and more,
    louder and louder,
    happier and happier.
She slid forward,
    leaned back,
    threw her arms and legs out wide,
    flung back her head,
and sang (showing all her teeth and tonsils)
at the top of her lungs—
long,
    loud,
        happy sounds.

You've got music in you, Kid,
    and it's fun!

A longer childhood can't be bad

Neat, Kid!
You get to be a baby
    a little longer than most.
I love watching you learn
    and seeing you become consistent
    in some of your responses.
A "Hi, Beffy"
is beginning to get a "Hi, Dad" back
    (even to Mom!).
A wave from me begets a wave from you
and, of course, putting you down again
gets a complaint
    that eventually will go away
    when something else grabs your attention.

You will be our last baby
and I must admit
that I like the idea of getting
    more "baby" out of you,
though I'm not nuts
about what that will mean to *you*
later on.

I do like the fact
that the "baby" in you
    won't quit so soon.
I do like that
    until I remember the other side of the coin—
the terrible twos
may last three years,
and (give us strength)
you may stay a teenager
longer
than we can bear!

Is there a storm in you?

(Seventeen Months)

They say that it's part of the Down's nature
that you are
what they say you are—
    a sweet, loving, gentle child.
I know that.
I see it every day.
But what I don't want to talk about,
    I'd rather not face,
    I prefer not to consider,
is that there may just be a whole other possibility
to you.

There are glimpses,
frightening glimpses,
of a storm just beneath the surface of you;
of a volcano just waiting
    for the right occasion to erupt;
of dynamite searching
    for a match to light its fuse.

When I see you asleep
and watch you love and play,
I see that peace
    is a part of your makeup,
and sweetness
is who you are.
But, child,
I'm always kept aware
    of the possibility
    of the suspicion
that somewhere, close inside, is a violence
    waiting to be turned loose.
Sometimes I see your emotions flip completely
    —an instant from cuddle to anger

like an on/off switch that changed complete light
    to instant dark.

And I wonder how far we are,
    you—and us—
    from destructive emotional eruptions
that through your life
will come and go—or worse—
    come and stay.

Just how thick is the shell
that will keep the sweet you
intact?

I find myself hoping
that what I see
is just what we
    (in our advanced years of parenthood)
have spoiled you,
and that what seems like a storm
is just a spoiled kid's normal reaction
to any displeasure.

That we can cure
    and we can live with.
But what if it's something deep,
    and with
    a hair-trigger?

Having a child at our age

(One and a Half Years)

Life just oozes out all over you, Kid.
Sometimes your life
invigorates mine
with a gentle touch
that awakens such good things in me.

Other times that life of yours
shouts out its presence with an exuberance
that seems almost illegal.

You do know how to fill a room.

Often,
when I feel the pressures
of facing the rest of my life
of rearing another human being,
it dawns on me that the option is
to spend that life
with a vacuum where you might have been.

In those moments,
I count things.
I count the steady joy,
the thousands of happies, the new purposes and challenges,
the hugs, the happy and tearful eyes,
the fulfilling and surrounding love
of you,

and I can't help
but thank God
for *all* of it.

Shoot, Kid,
we were going to be doing

something
with the rest of our lives.
Why not
do *you?*
It's sure better than doing life
without you!

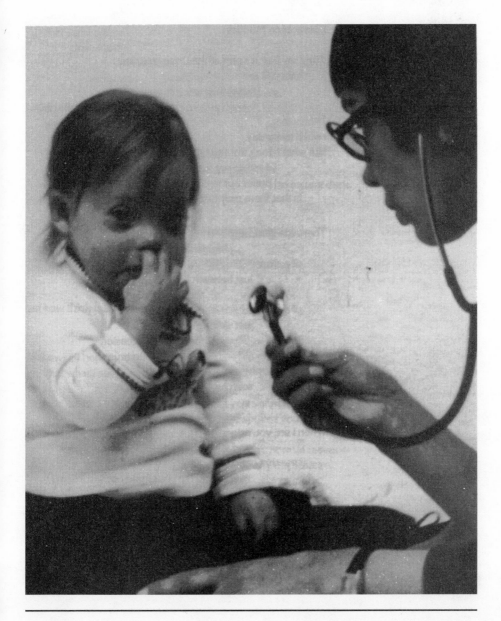

"But she doesn't look like Down's..."

"But I think they are wrong—
she simply doesn't appear to have Down's.
She's so alert
    quick
    bright
    normal…"

I never know just how to handle words like these.

On the one hand, I'm proud—
    proud that she's doing so well,
    proud that she's keeping up
        and so close to "normal"
    proud of the people who work so hard
        to help her stretch herself.

Yet, on the other hand, aware—
    aware that she *does* have Down's
and that nothing changes that.

I don't want to hide or disguise her Down's.
I'm not ashamed of it.
    (Yet why am I pleased when people tell me they wouldn't have
    known that she was a Down's child?)

I notice that
(especially if they respond well to her)
I *want* people to know that she's a Down's child,
so that they know what kind of a person she is,
how good she is for our world,
that she's not to be feared,
and that having a child like her is not to be feared.

I want them to know,
through knowing her,

that she's a person—
a real, whole
    field for us to keep planting,
    row for us to keep hoeing,
    crop for us to keep harvesting
person.
And a real, whole,
    planting, hoeing, and harvesting
person in her own right.

I want them to know
that this Downsy kid
belongs with our world,
    that she lifts with us,
    cries with us,
    laughs with us,
    contributes with us,
    and takes with us,
and that we need her
and all those like her
to round out,
sensitize,
and humanize
this world.

Music Therapy class

Five squat, little
Down's syndrome bodies,
with ten short, stubby arms,
circled in front of the mirror
listening intently
(almost too intently for 15-pound, 18-month-olds)
to instructions that they can't possibly understand
(can they?).

Bodies swaying and jiggling
to the beat of the music.
Shaking bells, tapping sticks, banging noisy things,
and loving the sound and the feel of it all.

There's rhythm in each one of you
    though certainly not a unison rhythm
    among the bunch of you.
Even so, you are a great little band.
I think we ought to sharpen you up,
    take you on the road,
    and call you
        THE DOWNS BEATS.

Hard-headed love

(Eighteen Months)

So serious
when your instructors
 tell, teach,
  move, and love you
into your tomorrows.

These are things you must learn
in order to function
 like other kids.
—No, in order to be *you*—
  and to be the *most* you that's possible.

So obstinate,
so hardheaded,
when their insistent "yes"
runs into your insistent "no."

You must get that from your mother.
You surely don't get it from a sweet,
easygoing guy like me!

Teething

How did you arrange
to grow your teeth
    here and there
    around your mouth
in the right places,
but in the wrong sequence?

You started fine—
    one in the bottom middle,
    then one next to it.
But then you went crazy—
teeth exploding all over your mouth—
    one in the back,
    one up top,
    another on the side.
And finally, they all came in,
    just right (eventually),
    beautiful, well-spaced, lined up.
I never thought you'd do it!

Now, if your tooth *growing* caused us some consternation
your tooth *testing* is what raised
    anxiety
in your mother's heart.

Nursing a kid with ornery eyes like yours
made her feel like a person
who would purposely stick her finger
    on a moving saw blade.

You didn't,
    we admit,
    use teeth as a weapon
until the second jagged razortooth arrived.

I remember the day
you looked into her eyes
and without wavering,
    without passion,
decided to test her pain level.

Your two teeth
sank into her nursing breast,
and that moment, that day, that second,
you brought an end
to your
nursing.

The most important thing is who you are

(Nineteen Months)

My daughter,
    who you are
    and
    what you are
is far more important than
    who you are *not*
    and
    what you are *not*.

All of us are *not*
    things that we would like to be,
and do not know
    things that we would like to know.

The difference between what *we*
    could be and know and do
is massive for all of us.

Your difference
is only
    a little more massive
than most of ours
in the total scheme of things.

And yet,
when it comes to potential,
you are probably
a lot closer to yours
    than we are to ours.

For you constantly try,
    persist,
    spend effort,
where we are more likely to coast,

relax,
and settle for less.

If effort produces greatness,
then you
are one of the great,
and I, child,
 am proud to have been given the gift
  of being your father.

How much do we push you?

(Twenty Months)

Can *our* performance
close
some gaps?

How much of who *you* will be
depends on *our* efforts?

Years ago,
they wrote off children like you early:
    —short life span
    —little accomplishments or mental growth
    —eventual institutionalization
    —lots of health problems
They called you "Mongolian idiots."

But you had a very popular retardation,
    and a loving, learning way about you all.
Study made knowledge about you easier.

So we learned,
    and found you to be learnable.
But, still, we're only peering through your dusk,
and it's only through persistence
    that we have come this far.

Child,
there's an uneasy tension
between pushing you

and accepting
    who they say you can be.

So we keep asking,
How much of your tomorrow
depends on our efforts
    today?

If we simply relax our tension
will you have lost something forever?
Will we have closed a door for you forever
    by having failed to open it at the right moment?
How can we know
    whether we are doing you love
    or doing you damage?
Should we force ourselves
    to force you more?

Should we pressure you more
    to talk, to walk, to eat right, to use your fingers better,
    —to listen and obey?

Don't you ever get to be
just a kid growing gently at your own pace?
Or must we make every act
(at least *almost* every act)
    a learning,
    correcting
    experience?

Damn!
I'd like—most of all—
    for you to be just a kid.
But I can't risk letting you
when I know that might keep you
from being
    just an adult
some day.

INFANT DEVELOPMENT CENTER

21 mos.

Beth attends the Infant Development Center once a week receiving education and physical therapy. Attendance is regular.

The following changes are noted since the last evaluation:

Language:
- imitates words inexactly
- uses gestures and other movements to communicate
- with prompting, uses single words to express wants
- follows the simple direction "give me"

Social:
- often clings to or pushes away adults
- sometimes cries when preferred activity is blocked
- picks up and puts away toys on request
- independently chooses toy and begins to play
- mimics domestic activities
- usually plays near other children, demonstrating limited interaction at this time.

Eating:
- feeds self with spoon—many spills
- chews well
- continues to need assistance with cup drinking

Toileting:
- fusses to be changed when diapers are soiled
- bowel movements are regular

Dressing:
- pulls off hat, socks, and other simple garments upon request
- cooperates in dressing by moving arms and legs
- attempts to brush hair when presented a brush
- imitates simple grooming actions

Cognition:
- finds the toy hidden under one of several cloths, when object is of

interest to the child

- familiar gesture imitation continues with consistency; new and unfamiliar gestures are inconsistently imitated

Beth is a 21 month old girl. According to the Michigan Developmental Profile, she is functioning at the following levels:

1. Individual Program Plan 21 months

Assessments—		Gain in 6-1/2 mo.
Language	15 mo.	4 mo.
Social	27 mo.	11 mo.
Self-help feeding	13.5 mo.	2.5 mo.
Self-help toileting	16 mo.	4 mo.
Self-help dressing	16–17 mo.	5 mo.
Cognitive	12 mo.	2 mo.
Fine motor	15–19 mo.	5–7 mo.
Gross motor	11.4–12.6 mo.	2–3 mo.

Beth cooperative through evaluation. Creeping independently, but prefers to scoot on her bottom. is walking holding on to furniture for 1-2 steps. Lowers self from standing to sitting by plopping on her bottom. All reflexes are present and normal for her age.

2. Staff Comments 21 to 27 mo.

3-14-78   Beth's sister brought her to school today—Mother is ill, During education Beth elicited "car" several times after verbal model by workel Beth attended 30 minutes without moving away from sitting table. Beth would pretend that she was throwing several times, but would not drop object.

3-14-78   Beth pulled to stand, 1/2 kneel on right into stand, independently. Resisted squat to stand. Took 1 step to right while standing at table. Little cooperation with other activities. Cried during tilting activities.

4-3-78   Beth began to warm up half-way through session. Some verbalizing but not spontaneous. Liked "Ernie" doll—hugged, combed hair and gave kiss. Completed circle puzzles but did avoidance behavior.

4-25-78   Mom sat in therapy session today to see if it would keep Beth from crying. Beth went through obstacle course once, requiring much verbal coaching. Worked on 1/2 kneel to stand and squat to stand, however, Beth continues to put more weight on right lower extremity. Beth creeps independently but will sit-crawl on smooth surface.

5-2-78   Mother's group. Talked about changes in feeling with time and excellent early care at KUMC. Family going camping over Memorial Day with other families with handicapped children.

5-30-78   Demonstrated some screaming behavior with play activities. Responded to verbal correction and stopped inappropriate behavior. Touched 4 basic facial parts on verbal command.

6-13-78   Beth performed obstacle course with verbal and physical assistance. No crying was elicited. Sat on tilt board with some assist to keep her on, would not stand or kneel.

6-13-78   Beth looked at approximately 30 pictures—naming about 5; actions with name.

9-11-78   Ambulation unstable at times with some falling. Standing from squat. Sitting from standing without problems. Left, right, forward protective extension elicited in sitting, prone, supine. Righthand dominance but would use left if prompted. Very curious. Much verbal communication—jabbering.

Labels

(Two Years)

Labels—
should we work to eliminate them?

The label "Down's"
immediately categorizes her.
It says things to us:
    retarded, limited, sentenced for life,
    unable to perform like us, not "normal."
It evokes responses
that cause people to treat her differently.

Playing with her last night she seemed
so like our other kids at two—
    happy, funny, teasy
    inventive, sharp, pesty.

We work to stretch her limits—
yet the label always reminds us,
    conditions us, screams at us
that she has limits
that many of us don't have.

So I have to ask,
are the labels part of the limiters?
Or are they simply a way of reminding us who she is
    and who she can become?
Do we use labels to force us to face her real limits,
the ones we know belong to Down's—and these alone?
Or do we let them put other limits on her
that she shouldn't, mustn't,
be hindered by?

If labels describe limits,
shouldn't we *all* have labels
that describe *our* handicaps?
He/she is:
    unable to relate
    selfish
    closed-minded
    brilliant, but not nice
    a turkey
    or lots of others.

If I had a label to define my handicaps
    what would the label be?
How would it affect society's expectations of me?
How would my label affect my expectations of myself?

How much did we sacrifice?

"How," someone asked at a parent's meeting,
    "do you justify the sacrifices?
How do you justify the extra money,
    time, effort, agony, and love
that retarded children syphon
from the rest of your family?"

The question caught me by surprise.
Even though Matthew (microcephalic) had been with us for years,
    and Beth was now a fixture in our lives,
    and Mom-Mom (with arteriosclerosis) had lived with us almost forever,

I confess I didn't think of them in terms of *our* sacrifice.
I do remember wishing
    things were easier for *them* sometimes.
But I never remember spending much time
wishing that things were easier for *us*
    as far as they were concerned.

Now that I think about the question,
it seems that the ultimate answer to that concern
    would be to hope for their deaths,
and we kept hoping for their *lives*
—continuing and as full
    as we could help them be.

Understand,
we were always faced
with the *possibility*
of their deaths
    (constantly, with the "Mouse"
    and eventually, with Mom),
but we didn't think of it as a solution.

I asked each of our other children
what they thought
about what they had to give up
for the "Mouse"
and about what they might have to give up
for Bethy.

They all responded the same way.
They didn't think of them in terms
of any personal cost.
They thought, instead,
of what they had received,
and of what the others had meant to them.

There was some slight difference in their attitude toward Mom-Mom,
but the overriding feeling was
that they loved her,
and that she needed us,
and that even in the bad days
we needed her too.

Maybe, just maybe,
our children's response to these special people
has to do with the tone we parents set
even before they become a part
of our lives,
and with the values we put on other human beings
no matter what their situation might be.

People are gifts—
and should be seen as such.

It loses too much joy
when we only concentrate
on the problems
that the gift
might bring.

INFANT DEVELOPMENT CENTER

1. INDIVIDUAL PROGRAM PLAN—STAFF EVALUATION
27 months

Assessments—

		Gain in 6 mo.
Language	24 mo.	9 Mo.
Social	28 mo.	1 Mo.
Self-help feeding	16 mo.	2-1/2 mo.
Self-help toileting	16 mo.	0 Mo.
Self-help dressing	19 Mo.	2–3 mo.
Cognitive	18 mo.	6 mo.
Fine Motor	23-1/2 mo.	4 mo.
Gross Motor	16 mo.	3 mo.

Parents' concern—Increase schedule to twice a week. Are not concerned about toileting unless staff is. Beth doesn't eat well.

The speech therapist describes Beth's receptive language skills (or what she is understanding) at the 24 mo. level. Beth can:

1. follow 2 simple commands.

2. select 2 named objects out of a group of 3 objects.

3. show body parts, toys, and items of clothing on request.

2. STAFF COMMENTS 27 mo. to 33 mo.

9-25-78   Beth was in education for 1/2 hr. with Stacy. She worked well for about 45 minutes, She and Stacy imitated each other in activities.

10-6-78   Introduced "me" with ball play and function or action cues with ball and car. Some crying with Mother in room.

10-16-78   Little crying today—good cooperation. Gait pattern improved with low guard of upper extremities. Good tilting reactions in sitting and 4-point position. Up and down stairs with better coordination using railing and minimum assistance by therapist.

10-30-78   Good naming of associated pairs. Tolerated well for tactile cues on hard palate and attempted tongue elevation.

11-6-78   Increased understandable verbalizing. Attempted balance beam and jumping activities. Increased cooperation.

11-10-78   Added "I like food" pictures with Beth naming object. Some difficulty for imitation of sounds.

11-13-78   Good fine motor responses—blocks, beads, pegs, storybook. Good cooperation on tilt board in sitting and standing with assist.

11-20-78   Continued imitation of isolated sounds p, b, t, s, with good response. Following directions.

12-4-78   Recorded naming pictures; good re-auditorization on playback.

12-11-78   Very cooperative today. Good attention to small motor tasks.

12-18-78   Group with Stacy. Excellent response for naming pictures and following directions for on-in-under.

1-8-79   Good attention span. Beth seemed glad to be back!

1-17-79   Beth worked on counting 1-5 today and identifying picture cards by object use.

1-17-79   Repetitive syllable drill with good imitation of 2 syllables.

1-22-79   Performed obstacle course with minimum to moderate assistance.

2-14-79   Worked at table 40 mins. Activities included: block/made train; spontaneous simple strokes with crayon, both right and left; Maximum assistance matching colors; Moderate assistance matching pictures/objects; auditory recall good with 2 objects. Very cooperative. Counts rote 1-6 spontaneously.

2-12-79   Good 2-word phrases; spontaneous speech becoming more intelligible; good imitation of 2-syllable sequences. Introduced yes-no concept with fair response.

2-21-79   Performed obstacle course 2 times in 4-5 min. each time. Propelled scooter board in sitting a short distance.

2-28-79   Seen for education alone—great! Beth remembered picture she drew last session was of Claudia (Beth's sister).

3-5-79   Continues with good responding for agent-action and action-agent imitation. Also good naming without visible cues and response to "what" questions.

Waking up to her own music

(Two and a Half Years)

Music and dance and feelings
just seem to explode from you.
In the morning,
    alone in your room,
we hear your soft, waking chatter.

You have lots of gentle things
to explain to your dolls
    and to the animals
        on the wallpaper.
Then comes the quiet singing—
unrecognizable tunes and songs.
You have a way of steadily getting louder.
We open the door a crack
    to watch and hear.

You stand, then sway.
Soon your arms are raised
high over your head
and, like a Hallelujah Honey,
your body moves all over the crib
and the singing
is at the top of your lungs.

Such joy is contagious.
Sometimes, just five minutes of you
    is worth the total
of the two and one-half years
of the pains and scares
    we sometimes feel.

You have a way of paying off—
of giving us more
    than we can ever give you.

Her glasses

So, Little Three Eyes,
the repairs to your original equipment
    have already started.

Your eyes didn't start their occasional wandering
and crossing until recently,
and they tell us
we've got to try to correct it now
before you get used to
seeing two visions
    and then tuning one out.
So,
we shift the flesh-colored patch
    (it makes it look like the skin grew over one eye)
from one eye to the other.
That patch, combined with the bifocals,
makes you look like a tiny,
    scholarly
    pirate.
Without those things,
you just look like
a cute little cross-eyed kid.

You are so good
about the patch
        that keeps your eye from drifting.
We know you hate it,
especially when it has to be ripped off.
You complain.
You let us know you'd rather not have to deal with it.
But you obey
and try to hold still.

You are almost as good
        about the funny little bifocals
which immediately get fogged
and blocked with fingerprints,
        cracker crumbs,
        jelly, juice, bananas,
        and badly aimed kisses.

Now and then we see
that you have taken them off
        and then
        the frantic search
        begins.
You cooperate about as well
as Bugs Bunny with Elmer Fudd.

So *we* hunt.

First, the logical places—
        "Where was she last?"
        Look on things—
        nothing.
        Look *under*.
        Behind?
        Nothing.
        Look *in* things.
        Turn things over.
        Check other rooms.

Check other floors.
Check other *countries??*

Finally, much later, after we've given up
(but not yet ordered a new pair), they are found!
in a wastebasket
in another room
or behind some boxes in the back shed.

The glasses *do*
make her noticeable—
that tiny little kid
with bifocals.
People stop and take a second look
and say things to her
and to each other about her
with caring smiles.

At first,
the idea of the glasses gave me some problems.
How could a doctor possibly know
what a two-year-old can see
or how clear the images were
at different distances?
Was he just trying to sell another pair of glasses?
What if his guesswork was off
and the glasses were wrong
and hurting her vision?
Jeanne took Beth to him
and was amazed, pleased, satisfied
with his technical skills,
ingenious tests, and unique equipment.
And the glasses certainly keep her eye from wandering,
and she seems to feel comfortable wearing them,
and she acts like she sees better with them,
so—
I guess they are doing her a lot of good.
We'll see.

INFANT DEVELOPMENT CENTER

1. INDIVIDUAL PROGRAM PLAN—STAFF EVALUATION

Child's Name: Bethany Bakely   **Entry Date:** 7/15/76
DOB: 6/14/76   **IPP Conference Date:** 3/20/79
Coordinator: Lee Ann Britain   **Recorder:** Susan Cannon
Persons Attending—
Child's Family: Rev. Don and Jeanne Bakely (Parents)
IDC Staff: Melanie Ryding (Speech Therapist), Susan Cannon (Physical Therapist), Joan Rosenberg (Early Education Teacher), Lee Ann Britain (Director)

Assessments:	C.A. 33 mo.	Gain in 6 mos.
Language	31 mo.	7 mo.
Social	35+ mo.	7 mo.
Self-help feeding	30 mo.	14 mo.
Self-help toileting	23 mo.	7 mo.
Self-help dressing	24 mo.	5 mo.
Cognition	33 mo.	15 mo.
Fine motor	23 mo.	2–5 mo.
Gross motor	19–21 mo.	5–5.5 mo.

Parents' concern: "The next step after here"

Long Term Goal: Placement in pre-school program meeting Bethany's individual needs.

Short Term Goals: (1) Increase block building, (2) Increase paper/pencil tasks, (3) Improve manipulation of pencil, (4) Increase balance reactions in standing, (5) Improve coordination. (6) Continue sound imitation and reinforce jargon patterns with phrases which appear to be uttered. (7) Develop auditory memory for following two-part directions and repeating two associated items. (8) Continue sound sequence imitation. (9) Improve dressing and undressing skills, (10) Improve toileting skills, (11) Continue improvement of problem solving skills.

Plan: Continue IDC for Physical Therapy once a week; Speech and Education twice a week.

2. STAFF COMMENTS 33 to 39 mo. of age.

3-26-79   Beth was sick last week. Beth refused many tasks by saying "no." After worker responded with "Yes," she would say "OK." Work was fair—Beth into playing games.

4-2-79 For first time, Bethany spontaneously responded with "Bethany here." Cues necessary for response to "what doing" with action picture.

4-11-79 Beth refused counting activities—until worker did them.

4-11-79 Good phrases associated with picture naming and locating 1 or 2 action pictures.

4-25-79 Beth's preacademic skills include: (1) Name numbers 1-9. (2) Name letters B and Y. (3) Name circle, triangle, and square.

4-30-79 Comprehension tasks for "what doing" with cues. Good response for big/little pictures.

5-2-79 Performed ball gymnastics with assist necessary to stay on ball. Beth sat on tilt board without assist and rocked self independently. Assist necessary on all-4's and in standing.

5-2-79 Beth recognized the following names: Bethany, Lois, Claudia, Mommy, Daddy.

5-7-79 Bethany getting noncompliant at times. Minor success by giving her two acceptable activities to choose from and letting her decide what to do.

5-14-79 Introduced Mother-Baby animal picture series; continues good naming.

5-16-79 Performed tumbling activities on mat-rolling, somersaults, climbing over barrels and wedges with physical assist. Attempted somersaults without assist—appeared to enjoy activities.

5-23-79 Worked on tracing shapes (connecting dotted lines)—minimal assistance given.

6-19-79 Imitation of verb(ing) with fairly good articulation.

6-22-79 Locating 1 or 2 action pictures with agent-action cues, then repeat phrase with good intell. Drill stereotype phrase "I see —" with minimum cues. Good intell. Locating objects on/under table or chair with minimum prompts.

7-3-79 Beth forgot glasses. Located animal, food pictures. Naming pictures with 1 action

7-6-79 Worked in a group for speech, education and perceptual motor. Named objects out of sight by touch and differentiated pictures of nouns.

7-17-79 Good isolated /s/w/ tactile cues on tongue midline and for teeth closure.

Liking herself

(Three Years)

You like you,
don't you, Kid!
You like what you see in the mirror
    at home,
    in department stores,
    in shiny metal table legs,
    and every place you see your image
    played back to you.
You play with that kid in the mirror,
    dance with her,
    cheer her on,
    try out faces on her,
and experiment with her eyes,
    mouth,
    gestures,
    and expressions.

You like your pictures
and what you see of you
in other people's joy.

If there's one thing I'd like to keep giving you, my child,
it's *that*.

I want to give you
    (as much as I can)
a life of being comfortable
with being you.
You have that now—in spades!
We, and those who know you,
make that easy.

But the moments are soon to come
when others will try

---

to wrench that feeling
away from you.
And we who love you
are going to have to work hard and fast
to make your joy of who you are
strong and solid
and thick and deep
and real enough
that no one can shout it
or taunt it
out of you.

Look, Sweetie,
I know we can't *protect* you
from what people
—almost naturally—
will say.
I don't want to build a wall
to keep unkind words from you.
These words will come.
They will be a part of living for you.
The question is:
how do I prepare you
not to be wounded by them?
How do I help you know
that what someone else's prejudice says
about your worth
is not the same as what God
and *knowing* people
say?
How do I help you feel as good about you
as God and the people who know you
feel about you,
rather than letting your attitude
reflect and accept
what some unloving people
might say or feel?

So far,
our enjoying of you
has set the tone
    for your acceptance
    of yourself.
And that will be sufficient
while you are surrounded
    by us and our friends.
But will it be enough
to get you ready,
    for instance,
for the first time
    that you get on a non-school bus
    by yourself?

Will it be enough
for the first time
you spend some hours
out of our sight
    and our protection
only with *others*
on your *own?*

Potty theater

I think the reason
    you are taking so long
    in going to the potty
    alone
is that you like the cheering
that accompanies
each success
while
your tinkling
is still a family encouraged,
    family accompanied
    activity.
Shoot,
I've seen that bathroom more crowded ..
    with more cheering
    and excitement
than we usually have
at a family birthday party.
I never saw anybody use the "potty moments"
    to milk
    as much applause
    as you do.
Cheering, encouragement, and urging lead
to one squirt
    which buys
    a lot of cheering and congratulations
    for you.
"Good girl, Beff!" "Yea, Beff!"
You smile—
    proud,
    looking from face to face
basking in the rewards
    that come from such
    great
    accomplishments.

Then,
"Gonna do a little more, Beth?"
—Squirt—
    More cheers, more applause.
"A little more, Beff?"
—Squirt—
    smile
        applause.
If the applause isn't quite up to your level of expectation,
you ask,
    "Beffie good girl?"
and we make the cheering
    right!
That's good
for the final squirt.
Then
you head off for wherever you were going
    before you got interrupted
    for your role
    in "potty theater."
It's a triumphal march
    for you.
Ringing in your ears are the cheers
and still the conversation continues
    as adults explain to the new arrivals
and they, in turn,
    offer their congratulations.

I think there should be an award
for "Best Potty Act"
    or at least
    for "Best Family Reaction."
We've got potential winners
    in this house.

Chasing Dad

"I gonna *git* you!"
That's her signal for me to shriek
"Oh, no!"
and hide in some obvious spot.

Kid, you run just like you walk—
    same speed.
The only way we can tell it's running
is that your face and arms run
while your body waddles
at its normal walking speed
    —just with more excitement
    than pure walking.
You must have taught Daisy Duck her style.

Eventually, as I did with the other kids,
    I let you catch me for reward.
But that's always the wrong thing to do.
It disappoints, disgusts, and even angers you.
And then it's your turn to say, "Oh, no!"

You don't seem to know what to do
    when you catch me.
You are different from the other kids.
    You seem more comfortable with the chase
    than with the catch.

But, Kid, I've *got* to let you catch me.
After all,
how long can a fifty-year-old man
run from a three-year-old waddler?

Negotiations with a strong-willed kid

Doubt is not your major problem.

When a choice is offered,
your mind responds
with the quickness, force, and finality
of a mousetrap.

Getting *your* decision
to correspond to *my* decision
is where the heads butt,
and where, I'm afraid, I'm going to spend
much of my getting-old energy.

It seems the only time your decision
is slower than a bullet,
    or more moveable than Mount Rushmore,
is when your computer mind
scans the air
and senses strong conflict with your parents.
Normally that doesn't bother you
    unless you sense
    that you really aren't going to win.
We notice that
if we want a "Yes"
and you want a "No,"
you negotiate.

You hem, you haw,
you ignore, walk away,
    change the subject, distract,
    point at this, suggest that,
    tease, cry, tell us you have to go potty,
    grab a book, watch TV,
    wiggle your eyelashes, giggle and run,
    use your cute, use your anger,

cry, con, explain,
jump in somebody else's arms,
jabber with enough seriousness that we think you really are trying to
tell us something, ask for a hug, a kiss, a drink

or all of the above—
or whatever.

They tell me, and I read in the papers,
that the Vietnam peace talks were tough.
Maybe we should have sent
only negotiators who had reared
three-year-old Down's kids.
At least *they* would have been prepared.

Speech impediments

The impediment
in your speech
is more obvious to me
    than it is
    to you.
You jabber on
without stopping,
    completely serious,
obviously enjoying our (your) conversation,
assuming (with no question) that I simply understand
    or agree,
telling stories of the day's happenings
    or of things you want to relive.
When you do get very intentional
and deliberate with your words—
    saying them slowly,
    loudly,
    in syllables,
you seem to do it more
    because you feel I
    have a hearing defect
than because *you*
    have a speech problem.
Sometimes you say words
right in my face
    patiently
    insisting
    forcefully
even holding my cheeks
and making sure my eyes
    are following your mouth.

Just like your teacher,
you do it over and over
    until you assume I have it,
    or until you give up.
Sometimes you tease.
You make up a word,
try to teach it to me,
    and when I repeat it,
    you break up in laughter.

INFANT DEVELOPMENT CENTER

INDIVIDUAL PROGRAM PLAN—STAFF EVALUATION
Child's Name: Bethany Bakely
Entry Date: 7-15-76
DOB: 6-14-76
IPP Conference Date: 10-25-79
Coordinator: Joan Rosenberg
Recorder: Joan Rosenberg
Persons Attending—
Child's Family: Rev. Donald and Jeanne Bakely (Parents)
IDC Staff: Melanie Ryding (Speech Pathologist), Lee Ann Britain (Director),
Joan Rosenberg (Early Education Teacher)

Assessments:	*C.A. 39 mo.*	*Gain in 6 mos.*
Preschool Expressive	33.0 mo.	7-1/2 mo.
Language Scale Receptive	40.5 mo.	1-1/2 mo.
Social		
Self-help feeding	36 mo.	
Self-help toileting	28–31 mo.	
Self-help dressing	24–27 mo.	
Cognition	3 yrs. 2 mo.–6 yrs. 0 mo.	
Fine motor		
Gross motor		

Long Term Goal: Placement in Public School Program when age appropriate.

Short Term Goals: (1) Improve dressing skills. (2) Improve expressive description of object functions. (3) Develop counting skills 1-10. (4) Demonstrate understanding of time concepts-today, tomorrow, and yesterday. (5) Increase number of quantitive concepts understood. (6) Increase vocabulary of understanding for item functions, category labels, actions, concepts (locations, size, shape, color, other descriptions). (7) Reinforce phrase structure and emphasize imitation of short sentence structure. (8) Develop short-term memory for following directions and repeating a series of two and three associated items.

Plan: Continue I.D.C. Integrated Preschool Class.

STAFF COMMENTS 39 mo. to 4 yrs.

9-18-79   Attending preschool II. Great day.

10-2-79   Beth did not follow directions well—stubborn! She pretends not to hear you speak to her.

10-4-79   Good responding during group speech in Preschool II. Cautious for tactile stimulation with shaving cream.

11-13-79   Toilet training going well. Good day.

11-15-79   Recorded N + is(ing) with reinforce of objective phrase and 2-part associated item recall.

12-4-79   Worked on Christmas decorations today. Began singing Christmas songs. Not as verbal as past sessions—maybe due to being absent for 2 previous sessions.

12-11-79   Beth very stubborn today—saying "No" to tasks and rolling on the floor during music! Toilet training going well.

12-18-79   Went to Santa's House—fun day!

1-7-80   Fair response for verb(ing) phrase completion; locating 2 or 3 pictures delayed, accurate. Sent home pictures for plural markers.

1-14-80   Beth into saying no! to activities and questions. She does well when activity is presented anyway.

2-4-80   Emphasized I want —, please with training cards with good imitative response. Beth appeared not to be hearing accurately as noted in /sh, ch, s/ production.

2-18-80   Very affectionate—did well on general information questions. Attended perceptual motor group.

2-29-80   Great paper/pencil tasks on pre-academic skills—matching number to number of objects and horizontal and vertical same pictures. Good attention.

3-14-80   Fair response for locating two pictures from multiple array. Good response for choosing category pictures.

4-25-80   Good day—attended well.

5-2-80   Pix for and assoc. with opposites up–down; hot–cold; day–night with good response for first two sets.

6-9-80   Beth required prompting to participate in majority of activities. Performed obstacle course and swinging. Refused scooterboard.

6-13-80   Good cooperation in class—did not want to go to PM Group. Celebrated Beth's birthday today!

6-27-80   Six month speech and education re-evaluation today.

Small but mighty

(Three and a Half Years)

How could so much love be jammed
    into such a teeny package?
You haven't got *that* much body.

You are little, small,
    squished, even.
And I don't mean little *because* you're a three-year-old,
I mean little *for* a three-year-old.
Yet you've got a personality
and a presence
that fills any room you enter.

And you've got a force of love—
    an acting, attacking, comin'-right-at-you love
that seems like it's more than enough
for a three-hundred-pounder.

When I look at you,
it makes me think
that, perhaps,
the One who packs love
is still trying to show us
    just what pure love is like—
how powerful a small cupful of it can be—
how far a little of it can go.

You see,
the world has had
its Einsteins, Copernicuses, Aquinases,
    Michelangelos, Moseses, Wyeths,
to make itself technologically
and artistically correct.

But to make it more *livable,*
God sprinkles it
    —sometimes stuffs it—
with those who love:
    Jesus, Francis of Assisi,
    Barnabas, Martin Luther King, Jr.
and a constant, always flow of kids like you.

With kids like you,
God gives us love
in its simplest, purest,
    least contaminated,
    least complicated form.
And it's the kind of love we need
    in this complex, tricky world
    of confused relationships.

And I'm glad God dropped
you off
    in my century
    in my town
    at my house.

Speech impediments (II)

How come things work
so funny with you?
Like the way sweat
    affects your speech.
It makes your glasses slip
down your face
and pinch
that nothin' nose
of yours,
and *that* makes you
    talk funny.

You are fun!

I know folks
would like me to use
a better word
to describe you, Kid,
but the word that
seems to do the job best
is *fun*.

You're *fun*, Kid.

When you wake up in the morning,
when your face and body run to me at the end of a working day,
when we laboriously go through all your play routines,
when you supply the melody as I sing you to sleep,
and even when you supply us with the wrong note
    to sing our grace at meals—
the word that fits most,
that hits you right on the nose
is
fun.

You bring a warm, lots-of-laughing
    happiness into our lives,
and that's called
fun.

Sesame Street

During "Sesame Street"
is not the time
    to try to attract your attention.

You are so mesmerized
that I have to turn off the set
to get your attention.

But Sesame Street does a job
and you remember
and learn
things that keep slipping back
    into your living skills.

So many people
    so many groups
are helping you to be
as much *you*
as possible.

And I'm grateful.

INFANT DEVELOPMENT CENTER

Age 4—5 yr

Excerpt of comments from progress notes:

Started new preschool group. Entered class with no hesitation.

Speech session and emphases on noun plus verbs with -ing endings.

Wore eye patch—to have surgery at end of month.

Beth needs maximum assistance to cut out 4" circle—pastes cut shapes independently. Beth recognizes and names letters A-Z.

Arrived in bad mood—says "I can't," but then was cooperative.

Beth completes worksheet and enjoys independent drawing. Beth does not return to preschool classroom, worker finds her in secretary's office. Beth answers "I don't know" when questioned about where she should be.

Cooperative. Followed group directions. Assist classmates in complying to directions.

Excerpts from Preschool Teacher's report:

Bethany Bakely was reevaluated in May 1981 to assess her progress since her evaluation in August 1980. Beth was cooperative and enthusiastic during the evaluation.

Beth passes all items through the five year level except one item at the 3-1/2 to 4 year level—Indicate number of halves in a whole. Beth recognized A-Z shown in random order. She is beginning to relate words she knows that start with the letters—i.e.: "B starts my name."

For summer, teacher recommends continuation of alphabet identification, number concepts 1-10 and continuation of number identification 1-20. Beth should be encouraged to write her name using upper and lower case letters.

Excerpts from Physical Therapist's report: Evaluated previously only in fine motor.

Fine Motor—Beth has difficulty with skills of tracing, coloring, copying and cutting. General manipulative skills are good.

Gross Motor—She is hesitant, does not like to take chances, does not use alternate feet on stairs, jump, hop or stand on 1 foot. Throwing skills are quite good. Equilibrium in walking is good, starting to run, although still a bit awkward.

Scores..................... *Previous* .... *Present* .... *Gain*

Fine Motor................. 4 1/4 yr......................... 5 yr. ....3/4 yr.

Gross Motor .... 4 yr......................... 4 1/4 yr. .... 1/4 yr.

Recommendation: Appropriate school placement.

Retarded?

(Four Years)

When I watch you, Kid,
when I see you move,
    and think,
    and plan,
    and invent,
    and con,
    and play,
    and procrastinate,
    and teach,
    and act,
    and tease,
    and listen,
    and cajole,
    and cry,
    and laugh,
    and count,
    and read,
    and love,
it's hard for me to believe
that a little sharpie like you
    is going to be retarded.

Listen to me—!
I even have to force myself to remember
    that the words "going to be"
    are already wrong.
The fact is, you always were
    always *are*
    always will be
retarded.

They don't have a pill,
    or a process,

or an operation,
or even a revolution,
that will make you
"un-Down's."
They just have ways
to make you less imprisoned by it.
But it will always be there.
You got it
You've had it.
You'll keep it.

OK—even though I know all that and accept it,
I've still got a problem.
The problem is
that even though I know you are retarded,
"retarded" simply isn't the word
that describes you best.
"Beth" is.
And being Beth seems so right
and so natural
that most of the time
nothing else seems out of place.
In fact, the only thing that seems out of place
when I'm with you
is the word "retarded."

When the word is tacked on to you
it somehow makes us stop seeing you as a person
—as Beth—a neat, natural kid.
The word turns us from who you are
to what you've got.
And who you *are*,
Bethany Flagg Bakely,
is more important
than any condition that affects you.

Learning to "sign"

(Four Years)

Derek, in your class,
has ears that don't work.

So your teacher, Joan,
learns to "sign" with her hands.
And you kids pick it up
as though it came naturally.

Your sister Lois
buys you a kid's book on "signing."

It amazes me how you remember
    the words describing the signs under the pictures.
You've got a remarkable memory.
I've noticed, though,
that the whole batch of kids in your class
    slur the signs
    just like you slur your speech.

Little hands and fingers zip
    somewhere near
    where they are supposed to,
and Joan goes nuts
figuring out
what you are trying to say.

Where's the "retarded" in her?

She's retarded.
Yet at four years
she knows her alphabet,
    small and large letters,
    by sight and by memory.
She counts past twenty,
    can tell me some larger numbers by sight,
    can read lots of words by memory
        (not by figuring them out),
    knows the colors
    and has words for most things she sees.
She remembers people and things from months ago,
    she talks, she runs …
    the list goes on and on.
So—where's the retarded?

Look, I know she *is!*
I just don't know, if she's doing
    all those same things other kids her age are doing,
just what it is
that sets her aside
and qualifies her
    for a special title.

Is she just a memorizer
—not a figurer?
Is she just a mimic
—not capable of conceptualizing?
No—she invents, plans,
    schemes, cons,
    responds, reacts, deals with.
Sometimes she handles life
like it was her own chess game.
She plans a move to elicit a response.
She manipulates actions and reactions.

So—where's the retarded?
She's retarded,
      but I can't pinpoint *where,*
      I can't define *what.*
She seems to have the basic equipment
that all the other kids have.
So—what's the key?

What is it that she's missing that will make her
      ever unable to do life "right"?
What *defines* her retardation?
What, finally, will describe
her lifelong delay?
      The inability to theorize?
      The inability to conceptualize?
      The need to always train and never coast?
      (Does the retarded mind lose information while resting
      like a pot with a small leak?)

Will it be that she just can't
      keep moving ahead on her own,
that she won't be able to take today's information
      and use it to answer tomorrow's problems
      and make tomorrow's plans?

On the other hand,
if she *does* have all the basic equipment,
can it be expanded to give her
      all the tools she needs?
Can all her equipment be trained
      to give her "normal"?
I see her with bright kids her age
and I know she's behind
in some things.
And I wonder—
      does she have *enough* of the stuff of life
      that with training, she can stay close to the others?

Can we force, train, teach her
into somewhere-near-normal,
or are there obstacles
that she just *won't*
be able to hurdle?

I catch myself looking for the right answers,
but I realize that I don't even know the right questions.
What is it, Bethy?
What's the blockage?
Where is it?
Is there blockage?
Is it all in you,
    or is some of it
    in our treatment
    of you?

No venom

(Four and a Half)

If,
according to our faith,
    love is the most important act of humans,
if love, in the end,
surpasses science and philosophy and art
as the key to making our world livable
    and our salvation possible,
if love is the key to life,

then how come kids like you
    have more of it,
    handle it better,
    give it more freely,
and then we call you retarded?

It seems to me
that if love is the highest,
    most intelligent, most curing
act of humanity,
you kids are the most perfect practitioners.

We are the ones
who seem more comfortable with venom.
You don't.

In fact,
    unless it's a very special event
    and you've been specially coached,
we don't hear "Down's" people say,
    "I'll kill that S.O.B."
or "Niggers are no good"
or all those other words
that spew poison into others' lives.
You are open about your feelings,

---

and honest about your thoughts and appraisals,
    and sometimes those things hurt.
But purposeful venom and hate
aren't normally the products of your personalities
    like they are of ours.

Maybe, Child,
we are the retarded ones.

Certainly
we are retarded
in the ability to give
perfect love.

The funnel
through which our love flows
is blocked by mistrust, fear, prejudice,
    and a battery of thought-out reasons,
while yours just flows freely.

Those who love less
    have always been threatened
    by the presence of those who love more,
and throughout history
    have tried to erase them.
But, Child,
God always has more of you to come to us—
    hidden in our genes,
    fighting, straining, waiting
    to make your entrance.

Yet with all its faults,
humanity seems to be somewhat educable.
So there's hope that someday
we will look at you,
    then look at us,
compare our love,
    and finally discover which of us
    is really retarded.

Communicating

January, 1981 (Four and a Half Years)

Listening to your endless chatter,
it just dawned on me
that something wonderful
      has happened to you
these last couple of months.

All last summer
when you rambled on at the mouth,
      people looked at me
      to interpret your meanings.

I could usually understand the first,
      and the last word of each statement,
but I'd have to guess the rest.

Today I discovered
that I understood
almost every word!

You are moving forward!
And Melanie's speech therapy
is paying off big!

The woman in her

"Hey, Pickle, gimme a kiss."
   "No, not now, I beesy."

I often wondered
if *that*
was inherited
in women.

Does it eventually become
"I've got a headache"?

Kid, you are well on your way
to becoming
a full-fledged woman.

Deciding who is worthy of life

Abortion is a big issue now.
And it has lots of ramifications for kids like you.
It causes me fears about the people
        and experiences
it may keep from our world.

The issue of a woman's body
and control over the life in it
        is an important issue.
But it's only the beginning.
We all know that lawmakers
could never let it go
with just
that issue.

We already hear them deciding
about the kinds of people
who should
and *shouldn't*
be.

And I don't feel that lawmakers are
        smart, kind, civilized, godly,
        mature, advanced, unselfish
enough to make decisions
like that.
None of us are.

In fact, I think
when history is written 5,000 years from now,
our times will be seen
        as an extension of the Dark Ages
because we still try to solve our problems
by taking away life
from those who are

or who might be
problems to us,
instead of capturing their worth,
opening their potential,
curing their problems,
and growing with the knowledge
and experiments
that come from loving and wise acts
toward the handicapped.

"If there's a chance that the child will be poor,
unwanted, abused, unhappy,"
some say, "abort."
Who knows before a child is born
what happiness he will have
—or bring?
Who knows
what her quality of life will be like
when she is thirty?
Who knows what cures will exist?
Child,
I too fit some of the qualifications for aborting—
born into a family which certainly couldn't afford me,
a family which became desperately poor—
and my life *has* been worth something
—to me and to others.

"If we know the child will be born deformed
or retarded
or handicapped…"
Beth, what they don't realize is
that what you have already given us
and taught us
is so much more than you can ever cost us.
Your brother Matthew couldn't talk or walk,
but he brought us more pure love
and taught us more about life and giving
than many of the folks who make the rules
that would deny life to people like him,

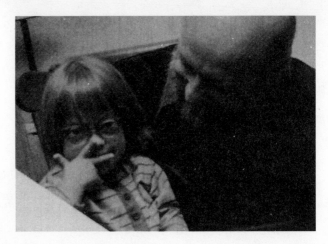

and would deprive our world
of a joy and a presence
that it can ill afford to lose.

And I'm not willing to trust decisions on life
to people who worry about how their decision
    will affect their chances for reelection.

"Handicapped ... retarded ... It would be better if she didn't live."
Better for whom?
    Her?
    Us?
How does removing her kind of love
    make us
    better?
How does erasing the challenge of a life like hers
    make us
    better?

Why would it be *better?*
Because she's not like others?
    No one is!
Because she's not as bright as others?
There was only one Einstein,
    one Schweitzer,
    one Beethoven,
    one Jesus.

Should the lesser of us die?
How should we decide which point of the I.Q. is too low
    for a valid life?
    40?
    50?
    70?
    71?
    72?
    What if we measured wrong?
    What if we don't have the right system?
How do we know, before her birth,
    what the measurement will be?
How do we decide which deformity
    makes someone unworthy
    of our civilization?

What about people who get deformities
    after they've been here awhile?
Do they *then* become
as unworthy of life
    as they would have been
    if we had discovered the deformity
    before they were born?

Look at us.
Humanity's history of deciding death
is a history of bad decisions,
selfish motives, and injustices.
    Jesus,
    Socrates,
    Joan of Arc,
    Blacks,
    Kennedy,
    King Jr.,
    Dachau.
We simply aren't good at it.
We aren't ready yet to make those decisions.
Who lives?
Who dies?

Bethy?
The "Mouse"?
Me?
We all fit into categories considered
    acceptable for death before life begins.
Please be careful.
You may throw away someone
    who could have given the world
    more than you did.

How will she feel when she reads this book?

(Five Years)

OK—a big question—
now that this book is coming to its conclusion:
    do I dare let her read it as she gets older?
It's no problem right now.
While she's young,
it's fun for her to know
    that there's a book about her,
and I can select from it what she can hear.
I can pick the poems
    that say love and fun.
But what about later
    when she learns to read?
She knows this is "Beffie's book"
—a book about her.
What about the poems
    that ask questions and express doubts
that she's not ready to deal with
    and maybe never will be?
Will these words hurt her?
Will they cause her to doubt herself,
    or pressure her into giving up
    on some aspect of her life?
How will she feel
    about the constant references to her
    as "retarded"?
How will she feel about so many strangers
    having access to her life?
What if she wants
    to hide her retardation
    as much as possible?
What if she wants to, but can't,
    escape this book?
Do I have to worry more
about what I've said in love,

than about what thoughtless people
will have said in ignorance or hate?

Will explaining to her
    that I only mean love,
and that I want to help other parents of kids like her,
and that I want that part of the world
    that sees kids like her as *strange*
    to begin to see them in *love* —
will that explaining be enough
    to make this book OK with her?
Will it make her proud?
    Or will it cause her problems
    the rest of her life?

I must be aware of her future feelings.
I must be aware of the possible good this book can be,
    for others like her, and for parents like us.
But I hope the loving tone we have already set
will continue to buffer her through the future
    of what good or bad
    a book like this might do to her life.

Bethy, I think you understand how we feel.
I think you already know
    that you have brought us joy
    and strengthened our faith.
And we hope we have done the same for you.
Together, child, we have helped
    to make each other whole.

To all who work with the handicapped

My hope for you, my friends, is this:
Each night when you look back at the labors of your day,
may you go to sleep with smiles on your faces,
    and memories of small victories
    in your hearts.
May the warm moments
you have given parents and children
return to you
    and keep the chills from your body and soul.
May the things you have poured
into the oceans of our lives—
    hope, joy,
    a clearer tomorrow,
    confidence, skills,
    small successes that cheer us,
    love, encouragement—
may all of these things come back to you
and engulf your lives
on each returning tide.

In moments when you wonder if it all adds up,
may you remember the success that you saw and lived,
but didn't know how to write
    into the proper spaces on the proper forms.
If I had two gifts to give you, they would be—
the ability to see where our children would have been
    if they hadn't had you,
and a good memory,
    so that each night,
    as the day begins to leave your senses,
you remember—
and go to sleep
    with smiles on your faces,
    and small victories in your hearts.

INFANT DEVELOPMENT CENTER

INDIVIDUAL PROGRAM PLAN-STAFF EVALUATION
Child's Name: Bethany Bakely   **Entry Date:** 7-15-76
DOB: 6-14-76   **IPP Conference Date:** 5-19-81
Coordinator: **Recorder:** Lee Ann Britain
Persons Attending—
Child's Family: Jeanne and Donald Bakely (Parents)
IDC Staff: Barbara Lawrence (Preschool Teacher), Lee Ann Britain (Director)

Assessments:	*C.A. 4 yrs. 11 mos.*	*Gain in 6 mos.*
Language	4 yrs. scattered to 5	
Social	Within normal limits	
Self-help feeding	Within normal limits	
Self-help toileting	Within normal limits	
Self-help dressing	not tested	
Cognition	5-1/2 yrs.	
Fine Motor	5 yrs.	3/4 yr.
Gross Motor	4-1/2 yrs.	

Parents' Concern:

Long Term Goal: Placement in public school program Sept. 1981.

Short Term Goal: For summer, recommend continuation of alphabet identification, number concepts 1-10 and continuation of number identification 1-20, Beth should be encouraged to write her name using upper and lower case letters. Suggest Beth work on address and telephone number understanding in preparation for school.

Plan: Terminate IDC Program in May. Attend local school system in Fall of 1981.

UPDATE—SEPTEMBER 1981

This month, Bethany Flagg Bakely did it!
    She entered kindergarten in the Kansas City, Kansas, public school system.
    She did it at the normal age, in regular classes—just like any other kid.
    As far as we know, she's the first Down's syndrome child to do this in Kansas history.
    She loves it!
    The tone set by her teacher, Mrs. Emma Smith, has helped her be a natural

part of her class, accepted and loved by the other children.

We are grateful to the Major Hudson Elementary School staff for taking a chance with Beth, and for making school such a good experience for her.

(Get ready, teachers. There are a lot more "Beths" heading your way. You are in for a neat challenge, and a great experience. You have the opportunity to make a real difference in the lives of a lot of handicapped children. Go with it! It's going to be worth it!)

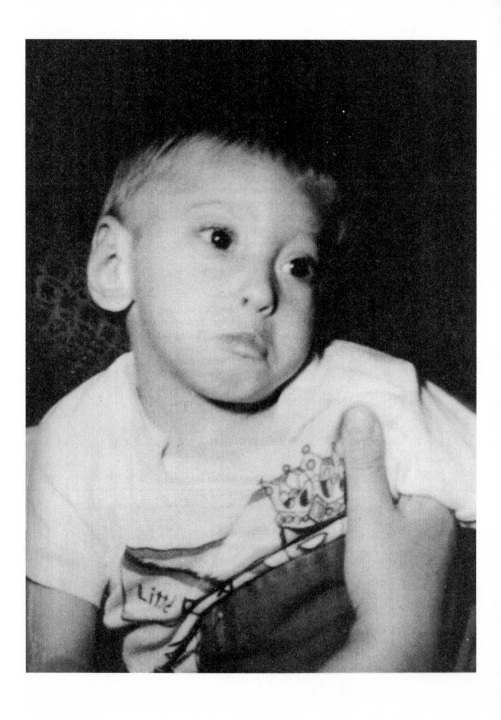

PART II

The "Mouse"

Matthew David Bakely

March 10, 1960 — September 7, 1965

So hard to write this

Writing this is a very hard thing
for me—
partly because I have lost too much of him
    from my head
and partly because the things I remember
    are the things
    that touched me most deeply
    and affected me the most.
Often, when I begin to fill pages,
    I stop.
Something in me cries,
"I can't do this."
"I don't want to live through this again."
"I don't want to feel his pain,
    see his tears, hear his screams,
    or watch him die—again."
I have already gone through that once—
in fact, too many times,
and it was finally going away.
I think,
    "Those who read this are strangers
    —people who have no right
    to want me to do this for them."
I think,
    "I can't possibly owe them,
    what writing this does to me."
But then, there's the other side.

I *do* write.
And when I do,
I get to see his face again—
    those big, always-saying-something eyes,
    that gushy mouth,
    that nothin' nose.

And writing and thinking,
I get to feel
that sweet, skinny body
    against mine,
those scrawny fingers
    squeezing mine.
I hear the laughter,
    see all that effort,
    watch the family loving him together,
and
    it's
        good.

And I'm reminded
    that I owe *me*
    him, again.
I need him.
And so do you.

God made him to be known.
    And this is the way you get to know him.
God made him to be remembered.
    And this is the way I get to remember him.
This is the way I get to hold my son again.

The birth of the "Mouse"

I missed his birth by a couple of hours.
    (This was normal for me.)
Jeanne was trying to be brave,
but finally it came out:
    "I think something is the matter with the baby."
We had a little warning,
but not enough to tell us any certainties.
—Jeanne had eaten some spoiled chicken
    while on a camping trip
    during the second month of pregnancy,
    and the poisoning was intense.
—This baby didn't seem as active in the womb
    as the first four.

The first thing that struck me,
when I went to see him,
was that he had dark hair,
like his mother.
    (All the rest were light,
    like me.)
Finally, I thought,
one for Jeanne.

Then I saw what she saw.

The head was distorted, flat in the back,
    like a chunk underneath the skull was missing.
There was just a whole different look about him.
My heart sank.
What are you supposed to *do*
    about something like this?

I wasn't repulsed.
I was just confused
about what the next step should be.

I never have had much of a panic point.
My mind almost always looks for the next move.
I remember thinking,
    "Well, we can't tell yet exactly what the problem is,
    so some decisions have to be delayed."
And I thought,
    "Whoever this is that God gave us this time
    must be someone God loves,
    and we are to love him, too.
After all,
    God has been in business a long time.
    God seems to know what He's doing.
And anyway,
    God seems to make decisions
    without checking with me first."
I felt there was a reason
that this child was sent into our lives.
    We'd just have to find out why,
    and decide what to do,
    as we went along.

I returned to Jeanne
and tried to be cute.
    "The first four looked just like me.
    The first time one looks like you,
    you want to call a specialist."
Then,
"Yeah, Honey,
    something is wrong.
    You can see it just by looking.
And the nurses all had it in their eyes."

So,
Matthew David Bakely—soon to be known as the "Mouse"—
was born to us.
And a whole new dimension was thrown into our lives.
And a whole new, wonderful experience
began to unfold.

They prayed for his death

They loved us.
They meant well.
One of the elderly women at the church
    came to me
    soon after the "Mouse" was born:
"We hear there's something the matter
    with your baby.
    We share your pain.
We are praying
    that this burden
    be lifted.
We are praying
    that your baby will die."

We loved them.
We knew they meant well.
But they came from a different age,
    a different frame of reference.
"Please don't," we said.
"You'll put God in a terrible spot.
We are praying
    that he will live!"

The guitar

The guitar
was his favorite instrument,
but that's because the guitar
    was what I played
and I
    was his favorite
    dad.
Each night, after supper,
    and before my church meetings began,
I would take him up to my bedroom,
lay him on the bed,
practice on my guitar,
and sing my way all through the "Simple Songs for Beginners" book.
He loved it.
    (He was about the only one who did.)
Noises were a special sensation to him
    and if there was *anything*
    I offered with that guitar
    it was noise.

If you want to plink and sing,
here's a couple of quick lessons.
If you are a good player,
    play loud and sing quiet.
If you are a rotten player,
    sing loud to drown out the guitar.
If you are a rotten player *and* singer,
    take your retarded kid
    (borrow one if you don't have one)
    close the door,
    and play and sing your heart out.

Look—
the kid's a captive audience
    (especially if he can't walk),
a non-critic
    (especially if he can't talk);
he probably enjoys the noise,
and you need the time together.

Hats!

Most hats are built to fit snugly
    on fairly round heads.
Now,
if you looked down on the "Mouse's" head
    and saw his head as a clock
    with his nose as the 12,
you would see a fairly decent circle from the 7 to the 4
but from the 4 to the 7, it was a kind of straight, flat line.
They don't make hats for heads like that!

But winters and rains and dress-up times
come to Matthews as well as to others.
And sometimes kids like him need hats.

Trying hats on Matthew in a department store
was often done with some of our other kids in tow,
and was one of the last great
pure forms of entertainment.

We would try hard hats, baseball caps,
    dress hats with feathers, fur-lined hoods,
    rain hats, shower caps,
    football helmets, baby caps,
    cowboy hats, and derbys.
And they would tilt to the back,
    tilt to the front, tilt to the side,
    fall down over his eyes, fall down over his ears,
    and sometimes over his chin,
    and do anything but stay on right.
We would tie them, sew on elastic straps,
    stuff the flat spot with hankies, or fill the hat with paper
    to make it only fall down far enough so he could still see and hear.
He'd push his head against the high back of his chair,
    dislodge his hat, which would fall down over his nose,
and he would giggle.

He'd sneak his head past the restraining guards of his chair,
   his head would flop down,
   his hat would snap off, and fall to the floor,
and he would giggle.

Finding a soft hat, with an elastic head band,
   with no stiff-parts-that-a-floppy-head-could-bump-
   into-things-with-to-knock-the-hat-loose,
   in his size,
   which looked good,
   and didn't emphasize his distortion,
wasn't easy.
But it sure was fun!

"Mouse" and the tough kids

When the street gangs accepted the "Mouse"
as a part of their lives,
       it was only partly a blessing.
They loved him half to death—
       which was good.
They protected him from harm—
       which was good—and bad.
He was surrounded by guard dogs.
If a stranger, even at church, looked at him oddly,
they wanted to do the stranger
some exquisite harm.
I had to remind the "hoods"
that Matthew *looked* different.
His handicap was noticeable.
It was natural for people to look at him with curiosity.
"After all," I explained,
"That's how *you* looked at him at first."

They finally learned not to take offense
       at those who stared.
I often found them patiently explaining
       Matthew's predicament in their own inimitable style.
Gradually, they learned through the "Mouse"
that kindness to Matthew, who was retarded,
should be extended to others who were also retarded—
       retarded in their information
       and acceptance of kids like him
       —and like them.

The "Mousetrap"

We tried to analyze his strength and coordination.
It seemed to us that he was strongest nearest his head,
    and weakest nearest his feet;
that he was better coordinated up top,
    and got less coordinated toward the bottom.
So even though he couldn't control chewing,
    his mouth was still the best coordinated
    part of him.

We often played a game called "Mousetrap."
We would touch his tongue
    with a finger,
which signaled his mouth to close
with the speed
    and the force
    of a mousetrap.
Same speed.
Same pain.

The finger had to get out immediately.
    If it didn't, and the finger got caught in the teeth,
    it was no longer a game to the owner of the finger.
Anything that got in his mouth
    got bit.
Always.

During these days,
Lois was an infant, still crawling.
    Matthew often lay on the floor, another object in her path.

Once, instead of crawling around him
    she crawled right over his tummy.
He giggled.
But on the way over him, her hand got in his mouth
and touched his tongue.

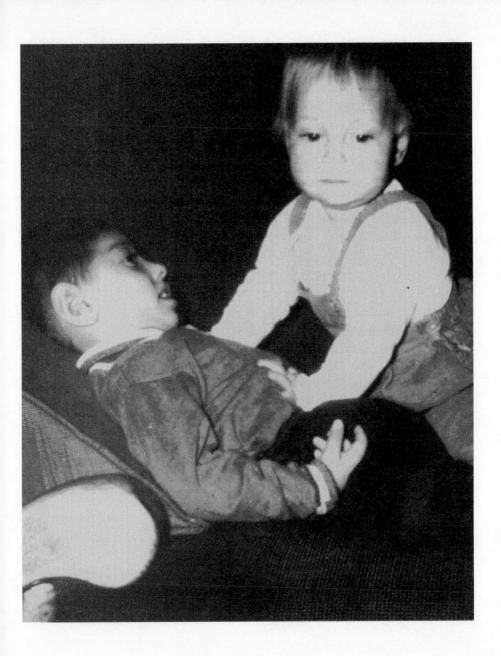

—He, of course, bit.
The shock of it more overwhelming than the pain
    (After all,
       other objects didn't bite her
       when she crawled over them.)
She quickly got off, sat up, and looked
    at this person who caused her pain.
Her bottom lip popped out,
    a few tears came,
    and she thought about it.

Then she went back to him,
grabbed his hand, and bit him back.

He looked at this person
    who caused him pain.
His bottom lip popped out,
    his eyes watered,
    he thought about it—
and he giggled.

Biting himself

His biting was uncontrollable.

Anything that got near his mouth got bit hard,
    immediately—
—his own hand, or mine.
Anything that got within range.
He didn't seem capable
    of *not*
    biting.
He had tremendous force in his jaws.

Feeding him was a lesson in patience.
He would bite the spoon
    and we couldn't pull it out.
We would wiggle it carefully
so as not to damage his teeth
    and talk to him
    to take his concentration off the bite.
Eventually we would get the spoon out,
    only to have to do it all over again.
Soft foods, ground up, already digestible,
    were all he could eat.
    Biting worked; chewing didn't.
Feeding took a while.

He had a certain chilling scream
that signaled a bite on his hand in the process.
He knew that it was going to happen.
He knew that there was nothing he could do about it.

That scream was the scream of anticipated agony.
    On the way.
    Unwelcome.
At that scream, everyone rushed toward him.
And we would see the thumb

on the way to the mouth—
his whole existence trying to force it away.
His mind screaming to his hand,
    don't!
His mind ordering his mouth,
    bite!
His eyes watching, panic-stricken.

Sometimes we got there in time
    and wrestled his hand away.
Sometimes we were too late.
    The thumb was in.
The sharp teeth met skin and bone—
the blood and pain almost more than we
    (and he) could bear.

His mind screamed to his thumb,
    get out!
His mind screamed to his teeth,
    hold on!
His teeth
always won.

Getting his thumb out was a work of art.
It had to be done quickly
without doing more damage to his hand
or causing him too much more pain.

I would wedge my thumbs
into the opening between his teeth
on either side of his trapped thumb,
    and twist slowly, but forcibly,
until his teeth opened far enough
    for his thumb to pop out.

The tears would continue
while his whole body
went from shaking
to limp.

Understand—
it wasn't something he got used to.
It didn't hurt him less than it would hurt you.
  (Try biting your finger hard enough to break the skin,
  and you get a small idea of what he went through
  several times a day.)
For a while, his hand looked like diseased hamburger.
We tried everything.
Tied his hand to the chair—
  but he hated it.
Pinned his sleeve to his pants leg—
  but he worked his arm out.

Finally, while patching up one of his many wounds,
Dr. Warwick (one of the world's most *decent* men),
  suggested a cast for his elbow.
It was the answer.

He could still move his arm,
  but not bend his elbow.
We would hear the scream
  that announced the hand on the way to his mouth,
rush to him, and watch
the stiffened arm move the thumb
  right past his face,
never able to get it into his mouth.
And the grateful, relieved smile
  would just fill his face.

Affecting the street gangs

"Hey, Bake, let's go!"
I used to hate driving the kids from the street gangs
    on their trips.
To get where we were going,
we always had to pass through downtown.
The kids would hang out the windows,
    say bad things to people,
      throw things at people on the sidewalk.
The van had our church's name printed on the sides.
All this didn't help our image.

One day, while baby-sitting the "Mouse," I found I had to drive
    the Pythons (who were as sweet as their name)
to the "Y" on the other side of town.
I got them into the van,
handed the "Mouse" to the worst of them and said,
    "Hold him—I can't drive and hold him at the same time."
The kid grumbled, but held him.
This time, as we passed through downtown,
    it suddenly dawned on me that they weren't
    hollering or throwing things.
I looked in the rearview mirror
to see what was going *right*.
They were all absorbed in Matthew.
They were taking turns holding him,
    kissing his cheeks, rubbing noses, and being gentle
with no shame or embarrassment.
The *Pythons*—the most vicious gang we ever worked with!

As I watched, it dawned on me what was happening.
For the first time in some of their lives,
    someone needed them.

A few weeks later, after a particularly tense time
    between the Gladiators and the Pythons,

I finally got both gangs to make a temporary truce,
and sent them on their way.

The head of the Pythons didn't leave.
He didn't seem hostile.
It just seemed as though he had something he wanted to say.
It was awkward for a moment,
    but, finally, he made his move.
"You remember that time you let me hold your kid?
Well, I just wanted to tell you
that was the first time I can ever remember
    taking another human body
    and squeezing it right next to mine without
    being smacked, punched, cussed, or shoved away.
Thanks. I know it wasn't easy for you
to let kids like us hold him."

I saw his eyes begin to cloud, and he quickly left
before he allowed himself the luxury
of vulnerable emotion.

My Lord, what have we done to him?
What is it like to be fifteen, and never be able
    to remember touching anyone in love?
    or having anyone touch *you* in love?
And who else but a "Matthew"
could have allowed him that one tender moment?
Matthew *couldn't* shove him away.
    His body didn't *do* shoves.
He didn't distinguish between people
    deserving or undeserving of love.
He was happy to be hugged by anybody
and to give his love in return.

Often those who look like they can only take
may have much to give,
and important things to offer
    to those who need.

Learning to walk

OK, Matthew,
we're gonna march!

Usually it was Steve, eleven years old,
who started the procession.
Six kids, parents, and whoever else was hanging around,
all lined up for homemade physical therapy.

At the thought of it,
Matthew's face and body came alive—
    giggly, quivering,
    jumping with excitement.
I held Matthew's body up
    supported by his hands.
Lifted his right leg off the ground.
Then the left.
    Then the right—
trying to teach him the motion of walking,
    feet rising and landing in turn.
We went single file.
The kids all playing imaginary instruments—
    trombones, flutes, cymbals, drums.
Noise, music, cadence,
    shouts of encouragement,
    laughing, cheers,
around the living room,
    down the street,
    across the park.
It *did* attract attention,
but the neighbors understood,
    encouraged,
    joined in,
    enjoyed
this effort to teach a boy to walk.

And he *tried*.
He wanted so badly to take his own steps.
Even we could feel the strain
    and see his desire
    to do this simple thing.
We knew he had no balance.
We knew his body couldn't control
    standing up or supporting himself.
When we tried, he just collapsed—giggling.
The strength was there;
    the ability to control was not.
But we felt that if he could learn to make stepping movements,
    someday the balance and control might come too,
    and get together.
And anyway, he needed small touches of success,
and we needed to be trying something
    —anything.

One day, as we were lining up for the march
and passing out the imaginary musical instruments,
    we saw it come over him.
Something started to click.

He,
    by himself,
    on his own,
    on purpose,
lifted his right foot off the ground,
put it down again,
and, of course, giggled.
And he *knew* that he did it!
We cheered, laughed,
    hugged him and patted his back,
    and told him how proud we were.
And he was proud, too.

It was then that we knew
that *he* knew
what we were trying to get him to do.
He understood!

It was an awkward step, of course.
He was so lanky and disjointed
    that he hit himself in the mouth
    with his knee.
The look of surprise on his face
made us laugh so hard
that we almost lost sight
of what had really happened.
Then Claudia said,
    "He did it!"
And the joy
    erupted!

He did it after that, too.
That right leg would go up and down,
and we would shout him on.
And when the day came
when he did the right,
    then the left,
we knew that he was on his way.

We didn't care
if it took forty years for him to walk.
He was on his way,
    and we were on the way with him.

Learning to love him

Being a family
active in the church,
we naturally had lots of meetings
where there were lots of people.
We wanted Matthew
    to be exposed to people,
and we wanted people
    exposed to him.

So we took him into lots of different settings.
(We couldn't very well leave him at home to answer the phone.)

Some folks at the meetings knew him,
    loved him, and dealt with him wonderfully.
Some folks at the meetings knew us
    and accepted him because of *that*.
But there were those to whom he was strange
and who reacted in accord with that feeling.

They would shy away, be repulsed, or just uncomfortable.

I would make a point of getting acquainted with those people
so that they'd be comfortable with me.
I'd bide my time, and at the right moment
    talk to them with Matthew in my arms.
Then I'd make an excuse to leave for a moment
and nonchalantly ask them to hold Matthew for me.
They couldn't very well refuse,
    and they couldn't hold him for very long
    without feeling differently about him.
And they often became the ones
who knew him, and loved him,
and ended up bragging
    that they were one of the ones
    who were allowed to hold him.

To the hospital worker who held him as he died

He had been sick for so long.
For two weeks the hospital could get
    no nourishment into his body.
For days and nights we held his frail weakening body
    and watched his painful crying become
    a weak, tearless whimper.
At nights we would go home
and fall into bed
    exhausted in our anguish.
The night he died
    was another
        of *those* nights.

We were at home in fitful sleep,
hoping that the next day of holding him
    would be the day
when his condition would turn around
    and start him on the road to health again.
So
    we weren't there
        when he died.
We weren't there
    when his eyes and heart
        needed our faces to say good-bye to.
We weren't there
    when his soul leapt free
        from his useless body,
when he finally stood—
    stood! on his own!—
        before God's throne.
We weren't there when our son's heart
    could no longer fight
        the overpowering force of death,

when it coughed one final time,
    and simply whisked him
        away from us.
We weren't there at that special moment of his need
    to hold him tight,
        to squeeze the fear out of him, and out of us.

We weren't there.
But,
    thank God,
        you were!
I don't know if we ever heard your name.
I don't know if we ever told you of our gratitude.
His death seemed to blot out
    all other happenings, information, concerns.
Our minds,
    our hearts,
were on overload.

But we've thought of you since,
    and thanked God for your kindness many times.
They tell us that when Matthew died
    you were holding him in your arms.
Your shift at the hospital had long been over.
But you stayed late just to hold our boy.
And he died in your arms.
Because of you, special woman,
he was able to move
from the warmth and love of your lap and arms,
    from the security of your face and your calming voice,
directly to the warmth and love of God
    without a break in loving.

Right now,
    I can't recall your name,
        but God can.
And I'm sure God's memory
    is better
        than mine.

I don't know
    if you will ever see this book
        or feel our thanks,
but to all of you
    who give your love
        while you give your skills,
thank you!
You have done more than you know,
    for it was you who made the transition
        from life to Life
a warm one
    for our son
        when we weren't there.

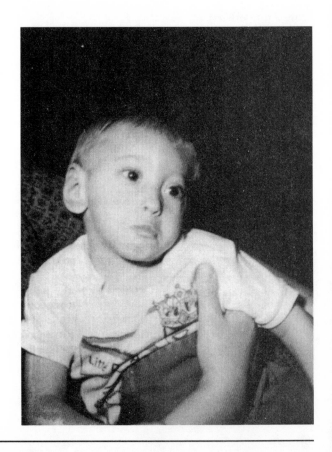

At his grave

I feel just a little silly,
    a little strange, a little theologically unsound,
standing here by your grave
trying to bring you up to date on your family.
But I'm human, Son,
    and humans seem to function better
        when they have something solid to feel and to see.
And this piece of ground
is where I saw them put you last.

Boy,
it's me,
your dad.
And I just wanted to tell you,
    to remind you—for your sake and mine—
that I still love you,
    and that the loving and remembering can't be stopped
    —hardly even dimmed—
        by a thing called death.
The thing I feel is the pain and the love
    twisting my insides
and making this moment, this act, so very hard.
I'm never sure that I can stand this.

I keep wondering if you sense me here—
    if this act, this gesture,
        makes any difference to you right now.
I almost feel your little body jump
    your little face explode in joy,
the way it did years ago
    when I would come home at night to touch you.
God, how I miss you!

If you only knew how I want to dismiss those years
　　between now
　　and that day
　　when your body and heart could no longer deal with life.

I wouldn't want you to go back to that kind of living again, Son,
　　but I sure would like a chance
　　to go through it again with you.
I need you, Boy.
　　I always did.
And I'm grateful—so grateful
to the God who was wise enough
to give you to us even for such a short,
　　blessed, agonizing time.
And I'm grateful even for times like this
　　—times that hurt,
　　but times when I can still see your face
　　and scrawny fingers
　　in my heart
and when I can feel your soul
　　and your joy
　　touching me again.
The want
　　wrenches me.

I want to hold that squiggly body
　　and touch my nose to yours,
　　and giggle at the funny words your eyes said,
　　and flip your body over on the bed,
　　and watch you respond to my guitar and my singing.
I want!!
Oh, God, how I want and pain
to be your holder again.
　　But I can't...
　　not for the rest of a lifetime.

Oh!!
God damn death!!
God damn it for the separation it causes!
God damn death
    for ripping you from this father's arms!
God damn death
    for keeping me from your face,
    for keeping me from those fingers
    that wrapped around mine!
God damn death
    for no longer letting me
    hug the pain and crying out of you!
God damn death
    for burning its way into simple human minds
    not really equipped to deal with it!
God damn death
    for this five feet of separation
    which might as well be a million miles!
God damn death!!

He did ... didn't he?
That's what the cross
    and the resurrection
    are all about.
Son,
    I know that your resurrection already is.
You are free from the body that trapped you.
You run
    and talk
    and laugh
and do the things your heart wanted to do
    but your body wouldn't let you.

God *did* damn death
and because of him, death stops being death
    and only becomes a wait for me.

Death/separation *forever* seems unspeakable cruelty,
    but death/separation *until*—
    I can live with *that!*

Yes, Son,
I *can* live with that
until I find *my* resurrection
and see you again,
and that certainly takes the bite
out of death.

I love you, Son,
    and death can never change that!
Love has a way of jumping chasms
and love doesn't have to wait.

Our need for kids like Bethy and the "Mouse"

The sad part is this:

if our society could invent people,
    neither Bethy nor the "Mouse"
    would have even been considered options.

And look what we'd have missed.

Postscript: Update on Bethany Flagg Bakely

At this date, Beth is 20 years old and in her second year at Kansas City Kansas Community College. She is taking courses in computers and in classes that will help her to work with handicapped children. They are regular college courses.

At the age of five, Beth was tested and found to be performing at a five-year-old level.

Because I (Don—her father) work with the poor, we have always raised our children in poverty neighborhoods. They all went to inner city schools. This worked out beautifully for Beth. In the inner city, there are kids from many different ethnic backgrounds, as well as rich and poor, smart and not-so-smart kids. Differences in the inner city are the norm. Beth, with Down syndrome, simply had another difference.

They started her in regular kindergarten, and she kept up. She went through her entire public school classes in the regular curriculum. The only special help she had was in math. (This was due to heredity, not Down syndrome. Both her parents were rotten at math, too.) She played violin in the school orchestra and sang in the school and church choirs. She also plays the piano.

In 1994, at the age of 17, she graduated from J.C. Harmon High School in Kansas City, Kansas—on the honor roll.

Today, she is in college, carrying 5 to 10 semester hours. College is tough for her, but she is hanging in there, and is determined to learn as much as she can.

Also, she is an assistant Sunday school teacher at her church, and volunteers each Wednesday evening to work with severely handicapped adults.

She, her siblings, and I are writing a book about her life, called *A Down Syndrome Journey ... Beth and her family tell their story.*

About the Author

DONALD C. BAKELY was born in a small town in New Jersey, the fourth of six children. While he was in grammar school, his family lived in poverty and Don had his first brushes with the law. After an undistinguished high school career, Don enlisted in the paratroopers, serving in North Carolina, Georgia, New York, and Alabama.

In 1948 Don heard the call to preach and was accepted at West Virginia Wesleyan College, where he attended for one year. He then served as assistant pastor of the Centenary Tabernacle Methodist Church in Camden, New Jersey. While studying at Temple University (where he received a B.S. in education and a M.Div.), he served two other Camden churches.

In 1958 Don was called to return to Centenary Tabernacle in Camden, this time as its pastor. This church had dropped in membership from over seven hundred to seventy, as the neighborhood changed economically and racially. Don's work included work with neighborhood youth who were involved in gangs.

In 1965 Don, his wife Jeanne, and their six children moved to Kansas City where he became executive director of Cross-Lines Cooperative Council. Cross-Lines helps people of different races and religious backgrounds pool their resources to meet problems caused by poverty and ignorance. Backed by several hundred churches of over thirty denominations, Cross-Lines involves many volunteers in projects that deal with housing, health, legal aid, recreation, community organization, job training, etc.

Because the ideas of Cross-Lines are workable in rural, city, and suburban areas, Rev. Bakely speaks on the average of two hundred to three hundred times a year across the nation to national, regional, and local groups interested in using their resources to meet community needs. He has received special commendations from President Ford, from the national Jaycees and many state Jaycee chapters as well as from other state and local groups. He was the recipient of the Liberty Bell Award from the American Bar Association and a life membership to PTA.

His first book, *If ... a Big Word with the Poor*, was free verse with photographs by Terry Evans, a Salina, Kansas, photographer. Don is currently working on another book about Cross-Lines, poverty, and inner-city work.